THE BALCONIES OF NEW ORLEANS

by

LAURA HAWKS

THE BALCONIES OF NEW ORLEANS

Whenever I go to New Orleans, regardless of how many times I've been there, I continuously find myself looking up at the balconies of the French Quarter fascinated with the iconic, delicate filigree, and lacy scroll work which inspires a sense of romance and awe.

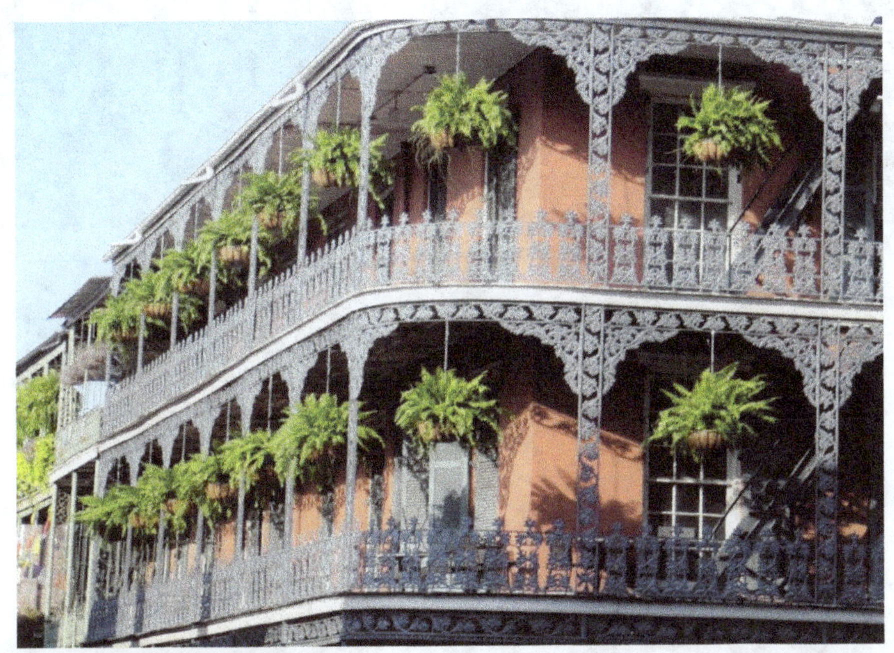

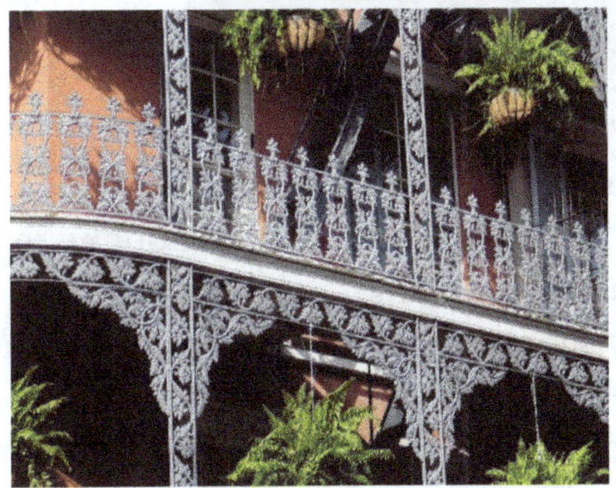

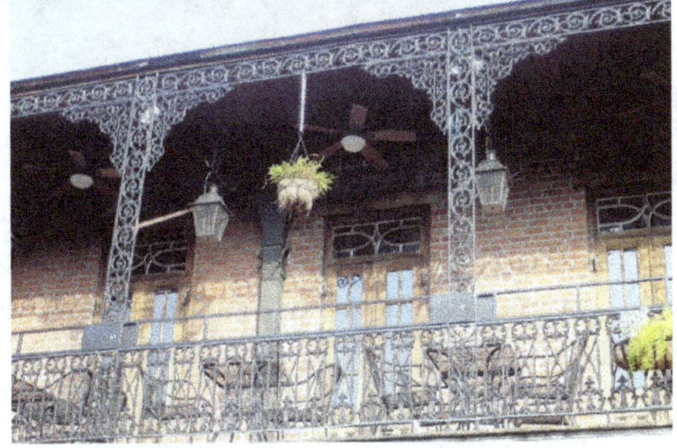

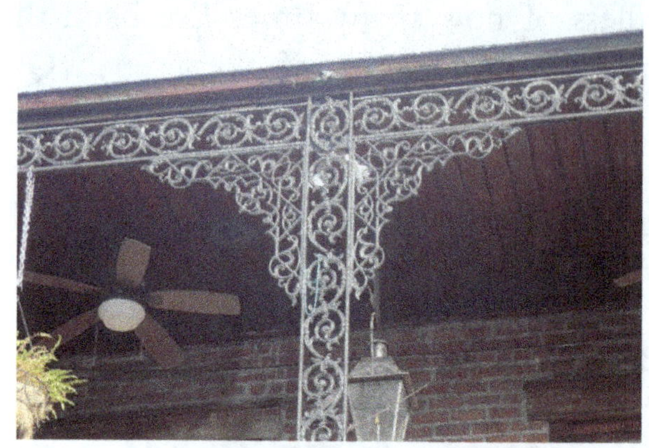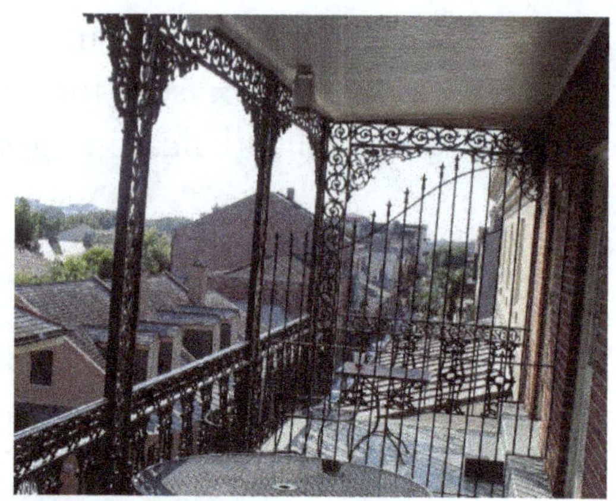

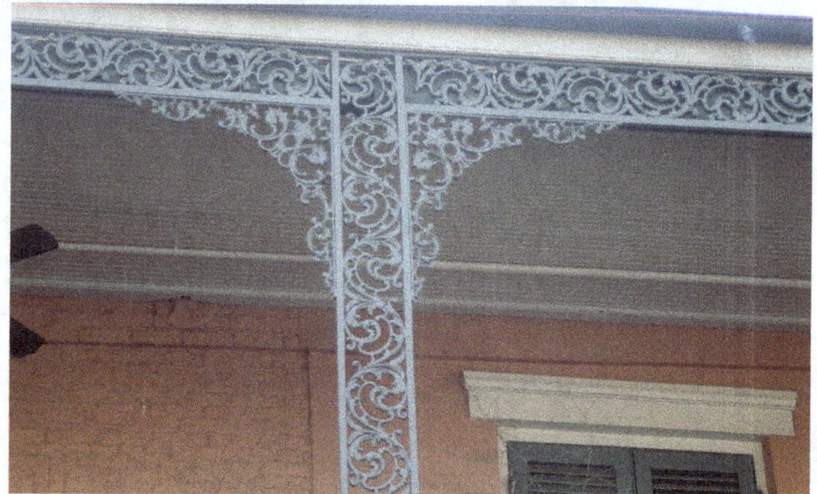

Snail Shell

Although balconies make the majority of what catches my attention, the ironwork on fences, doors, windows and gateposts also elicit a feeling of beauty along with great amazement for such detailed work. From romantic, lacy filigree to Fleur de Lis, from stylized crosses to curved waves and almost everything in between, one can enjoy the feel of almost stepping back in time with the quality and pride of the blacksmiths of old and the hard work of hammering out the intricate designs from the intensely heated metal as they plied it into a multitude of shapes and designs.

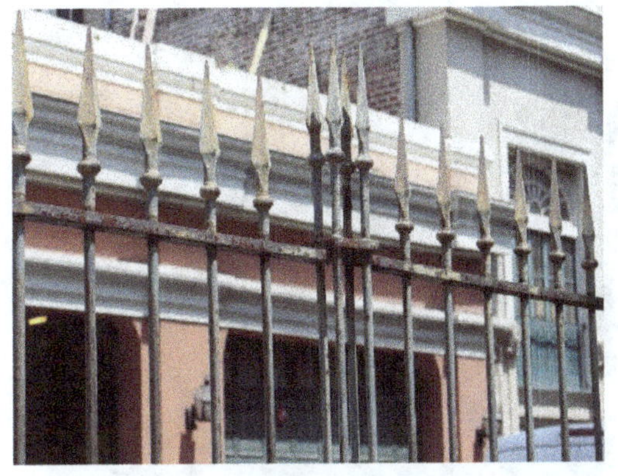

(Left): Spears

(Right) Texas Stars with open C&S scrollwork

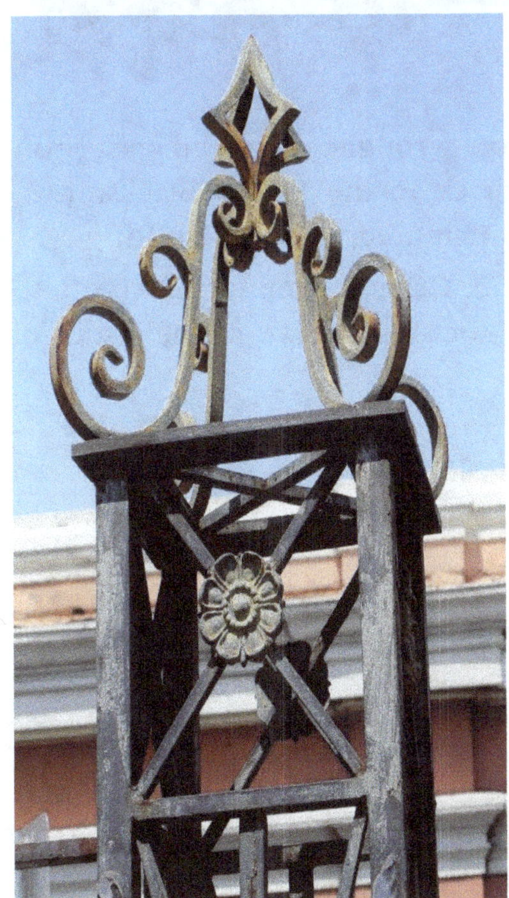

(Left) Gate Post

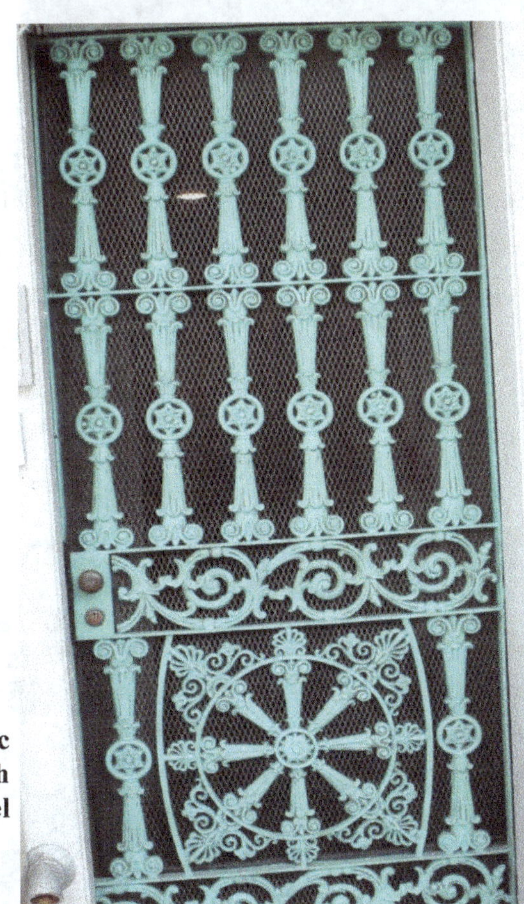

(Right) Greek Ionic Revival Pillars with star wheel

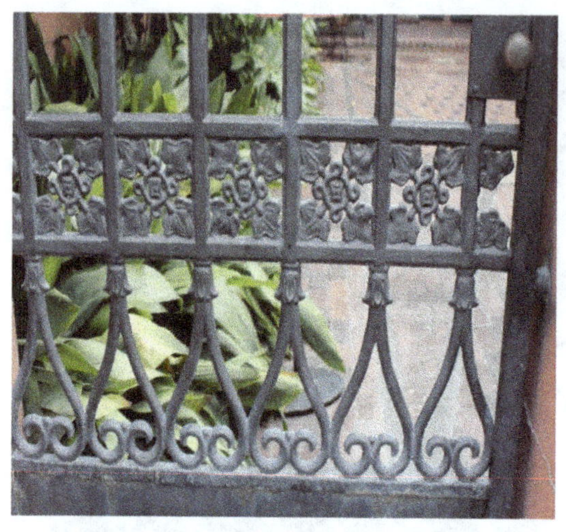

New Orleans French Quarter has more pieces of wrought iron and cast iron than anywhere else in the United States dating back to the 1850's. Blacksmiths, both free and slave, Europeans and Creoles all contributed to the everlasting beauty of iron decoration. There is no place in the Vieux Carre, meaning old city, also known as the French Quarter, where one can go and not stop in awe at the results of those who left such an indelible mark upon the area.

Open C scrollwork made popular in 13th century France.

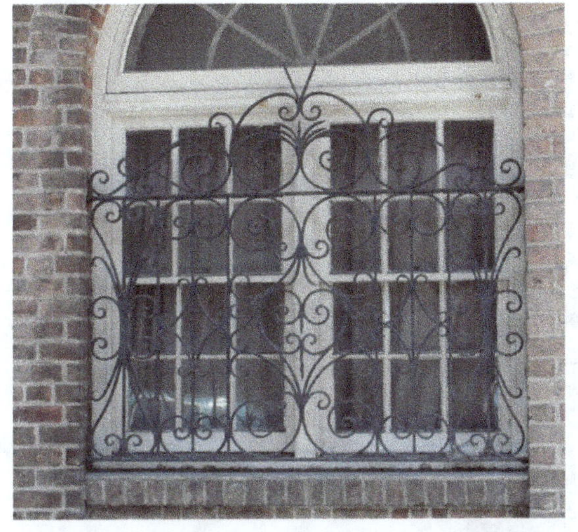

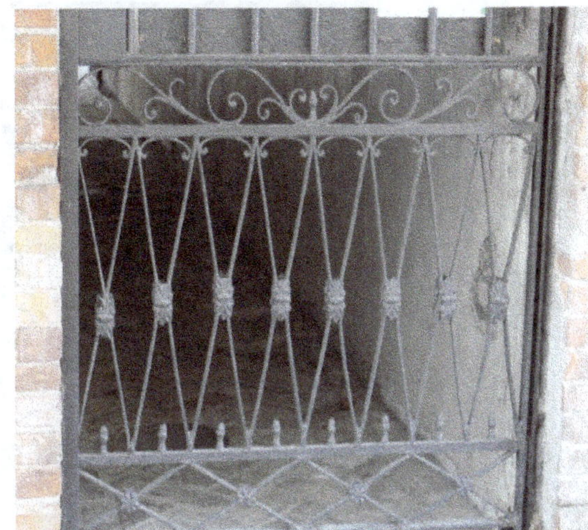

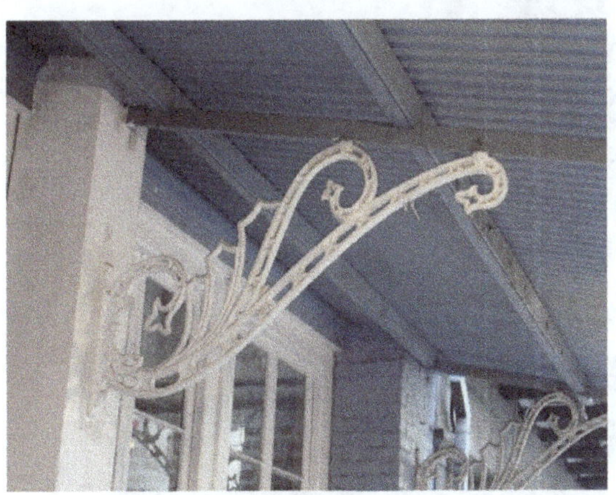

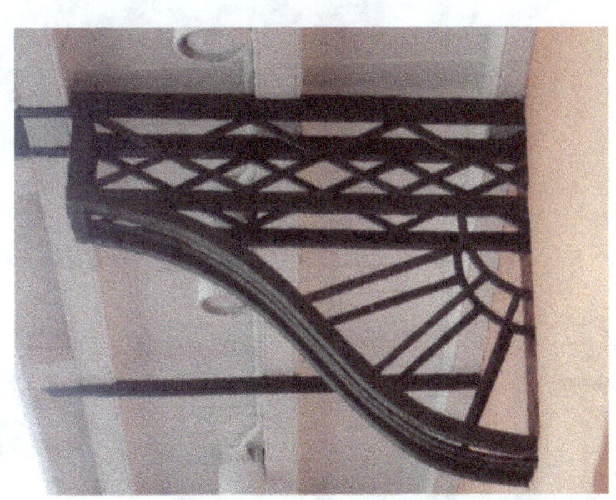

The images gained as one strolls about the old city can last a lifetime. How often does one stand and just gaze upon the work displayed for all to see? How many photos are captured in a multitude of pictures taken throughout the decades and changing little from one era to the next?

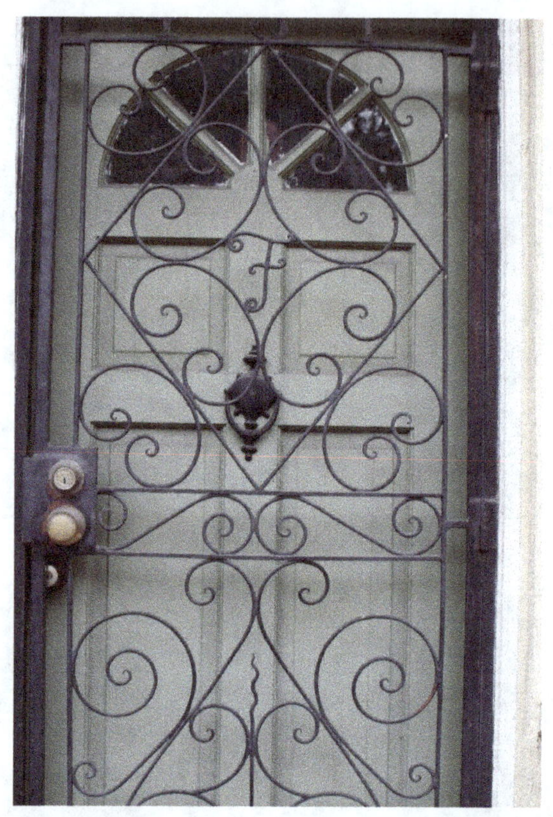

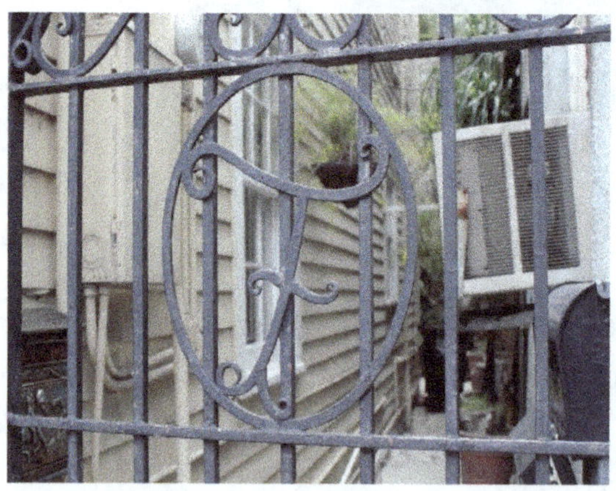

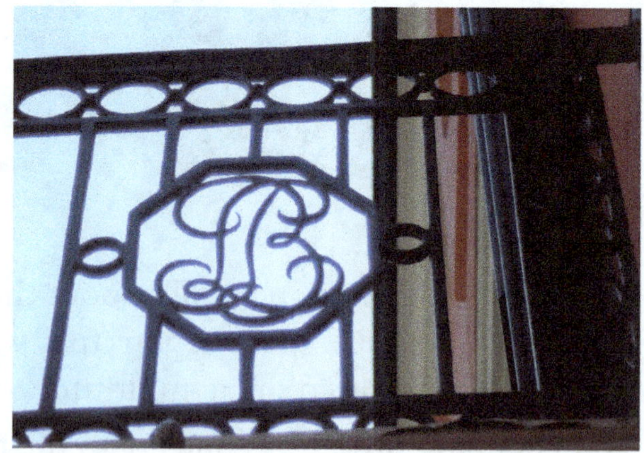

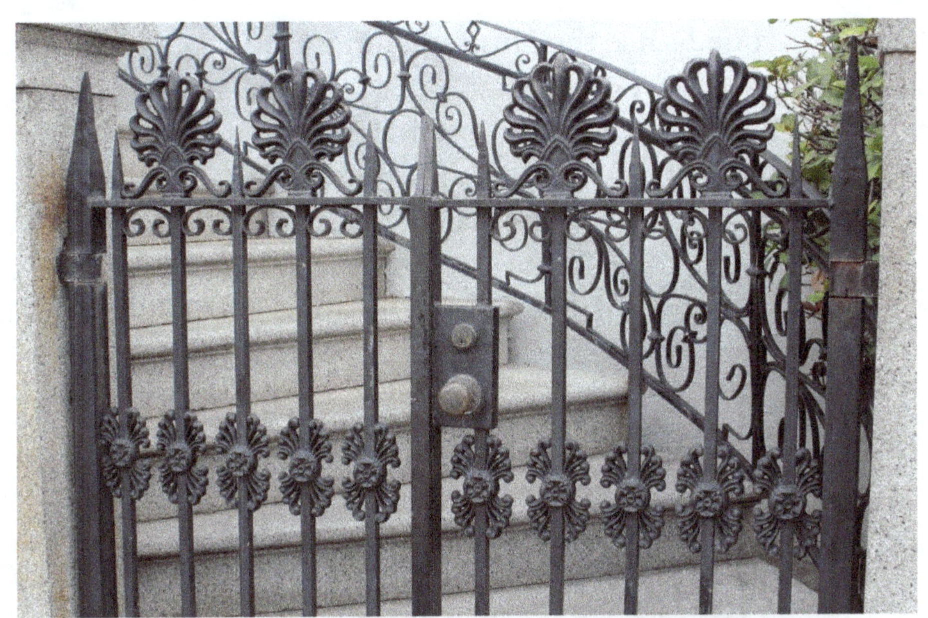

Dogwood Flower inset between a fan design called a repousse.

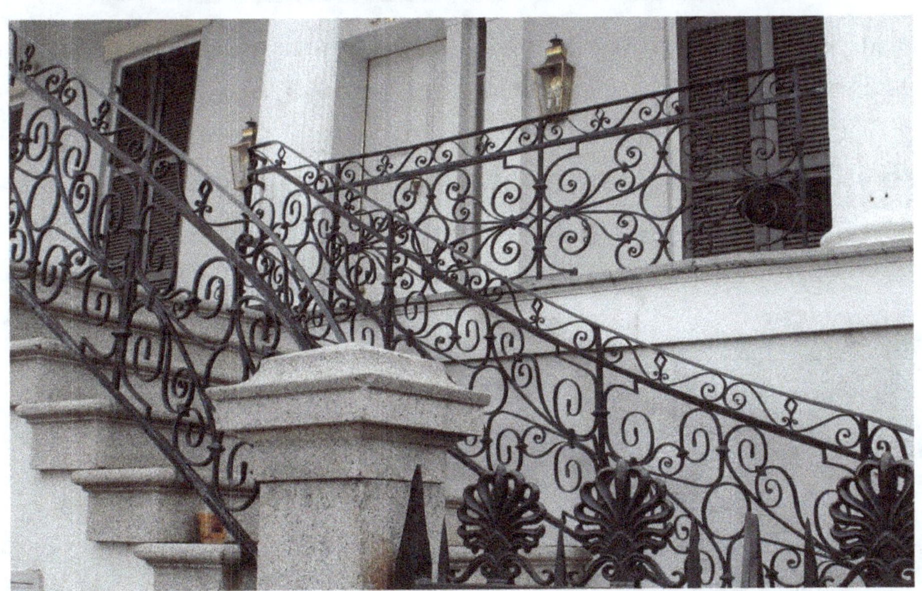

Ironwork has been around since the Hittites, about 1500 bc, in mostly utilitarian forms such as knives, daggers, swords and some small ornamental figures. However, it was the Spanish and the French who inspired the more noticeably intricate work of iron in the 1700's and 1800's. The use of iron for more decorative purposes arose when it was used to protect doors and windows from raider's attacks, especially in buildings containing gold and silver such as might be found at religious sites. In particular, this form of decoration became highly ornate during the Baroque and Rococo (Late Baroque) periods.

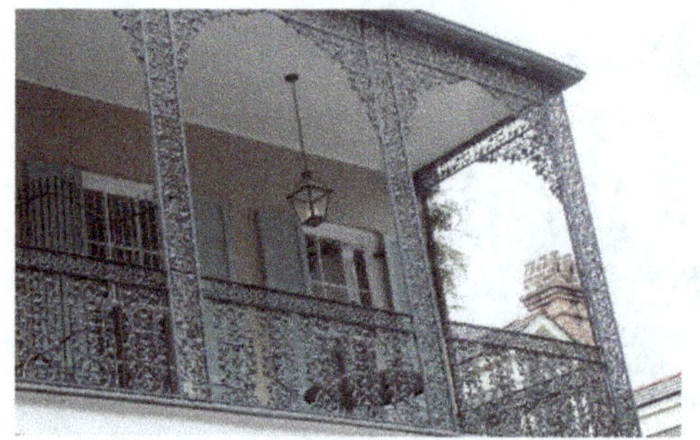

In Spain, elaborate screens were built in all of the Spanish cathedrals. It mimics another Spanish product: lace. In France, they used the decorative iron in places such as Notre Dame de Paris, Rodez Cathedral, the Palace of Versailles as well as many other French buildings. The English also utilized the elaborate ironwork in their cathedrals, such as Canterbury and Winchester. The delicate workings of molding iron were forged and formed into beautiful designs, some secular and some religious.

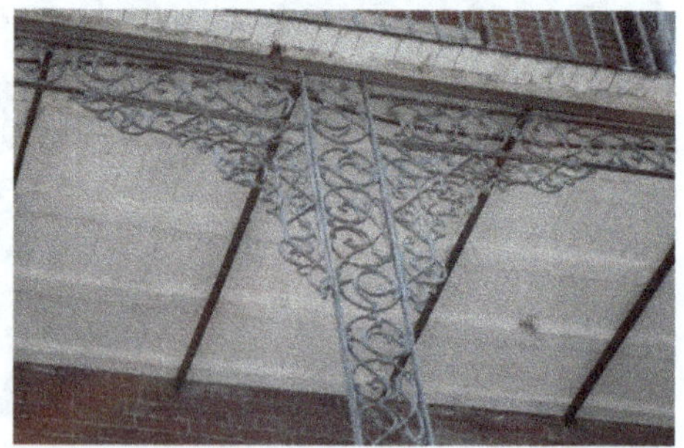

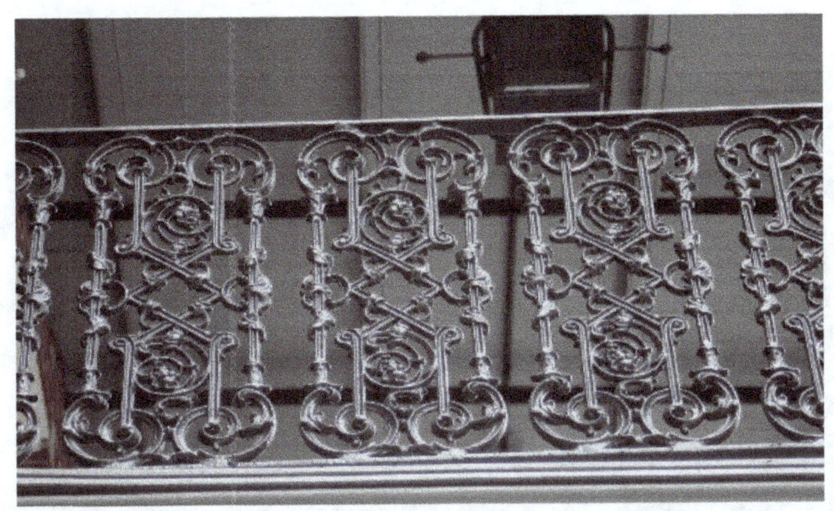

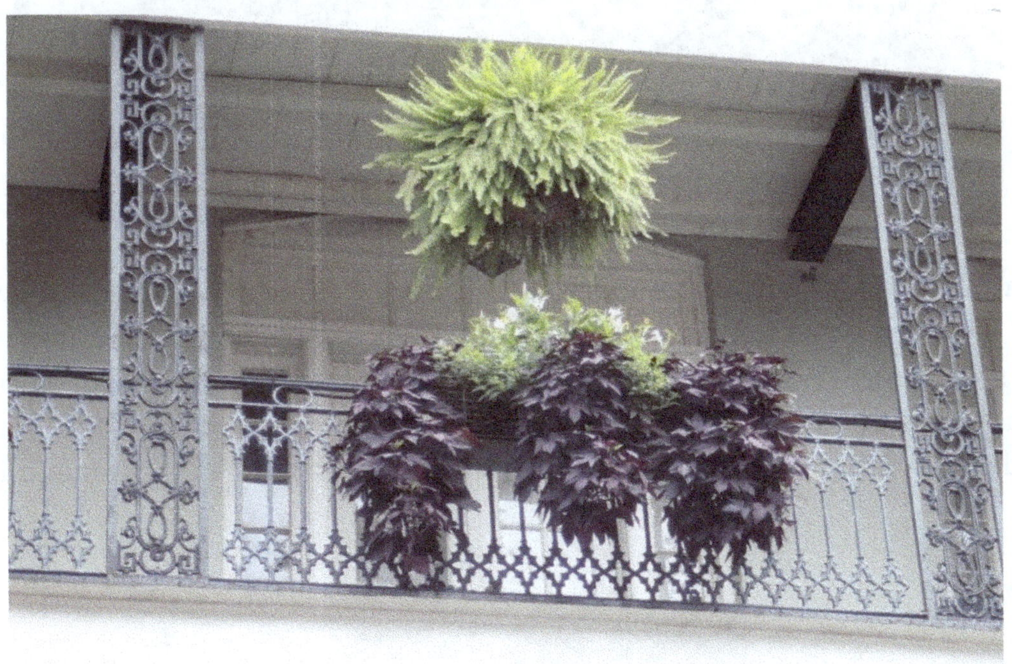

Stylized Crosses on Bars

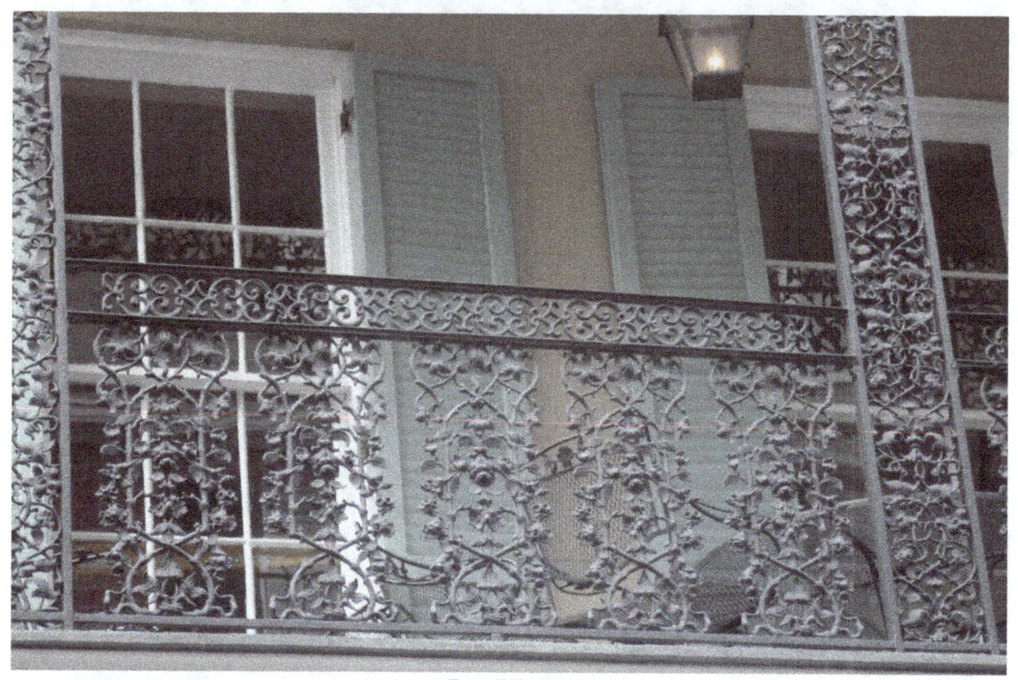

Ivy Vines

There are two kinds of iron work. Wrought is an old English term meaning worked by hand. This determination was usually done by blacksmiths who learned to melt the iron, then using an anvil and hammer to work the softened metal to form various shapes and designs. Wrought iron becomes more malleable the more it is worked and can be heated and re-heated. In fact, the more wrought iron is worked, the stronger it becomes.

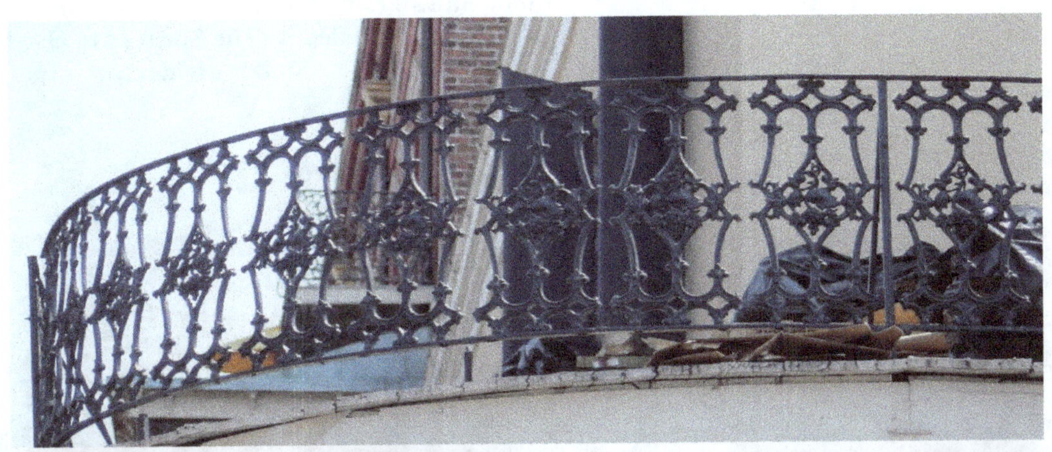

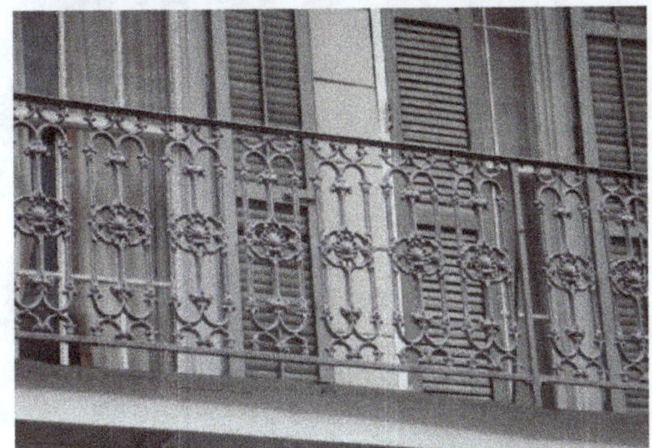

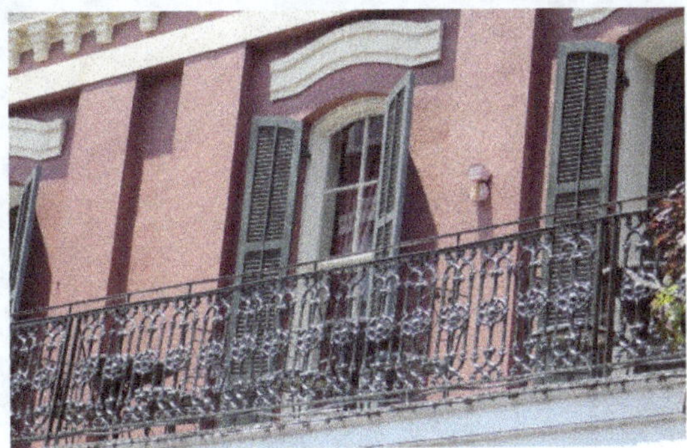

(Top) Notice the arches which encase the Seashells; seen on both buildings

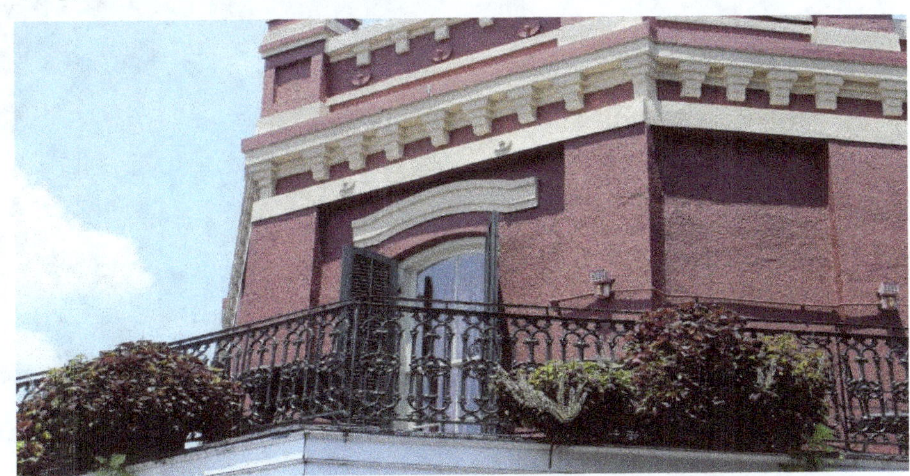

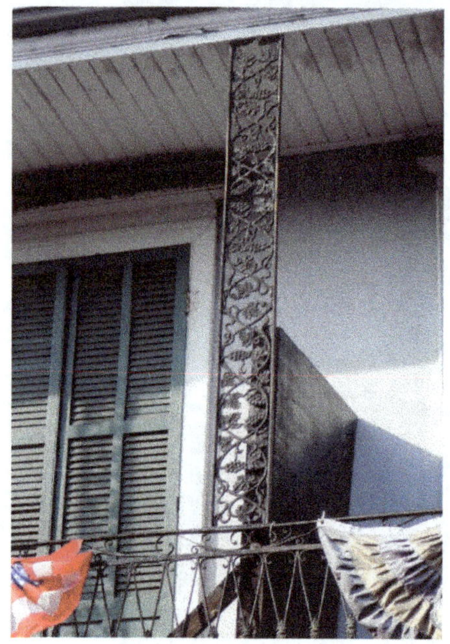

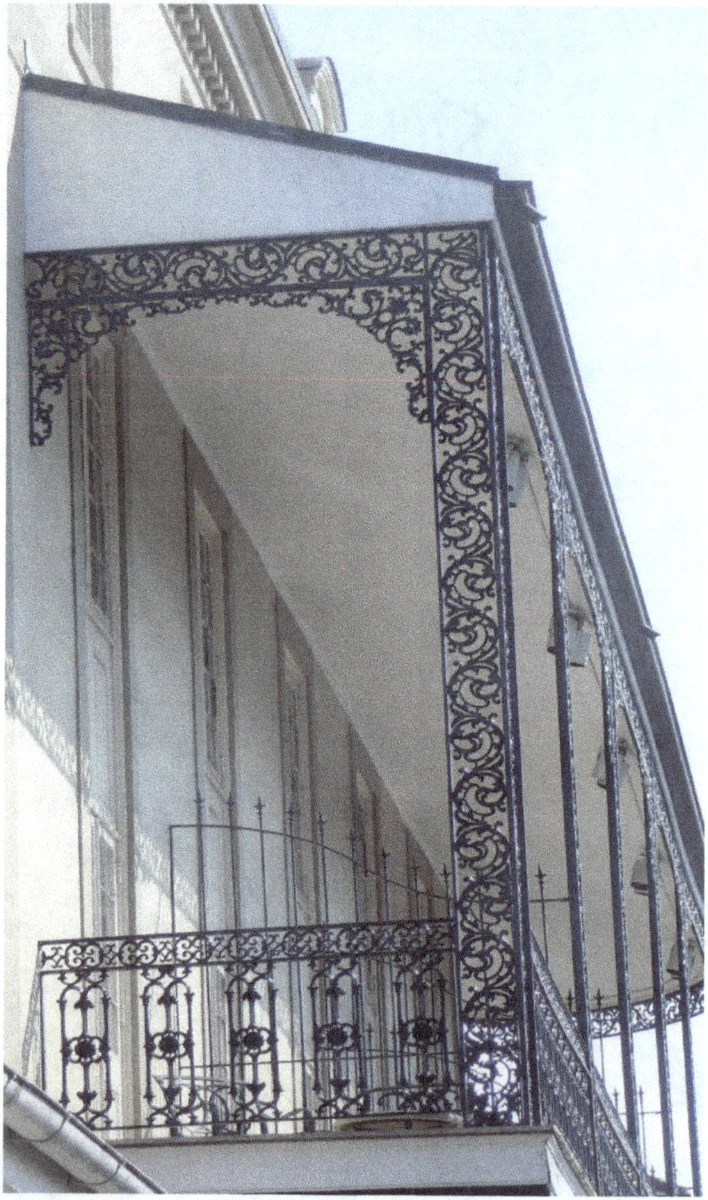

By the 1500's, iron's composition was slightly altered by adding additional minerals to it, such as scrap metals and various other alloy ingredients. Once melted, cast iron is then poured into a mold to set. As a result, it is not as malleable as wrought iron since it isn't heated and reheated. Because it's not a purer form of iron, its ore is more affordable and cost effective, thereby becoming more readily available.

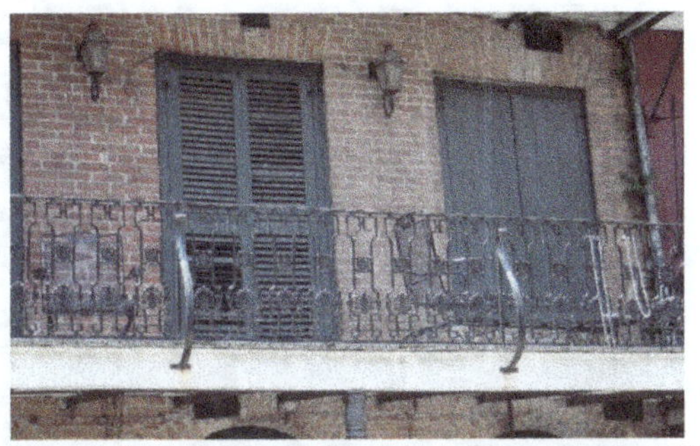
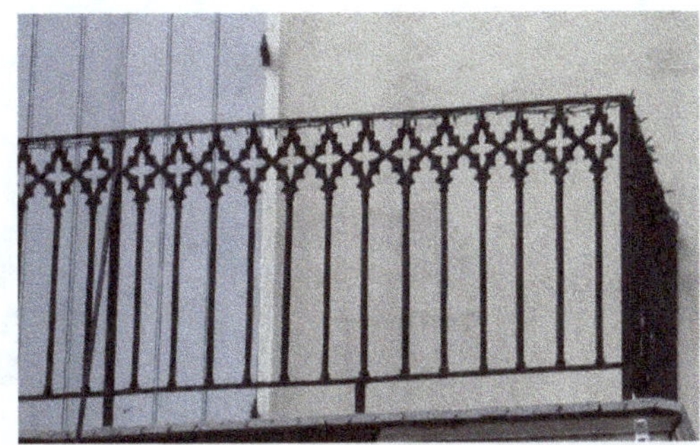

Spanish pantaloons balustrade support Gothic quatrefois with a simple bar

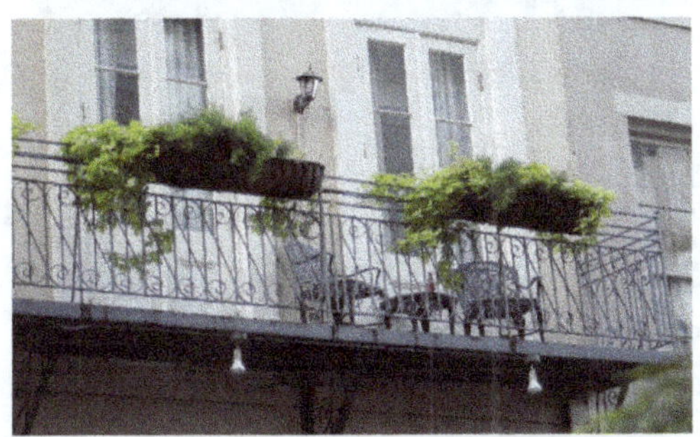
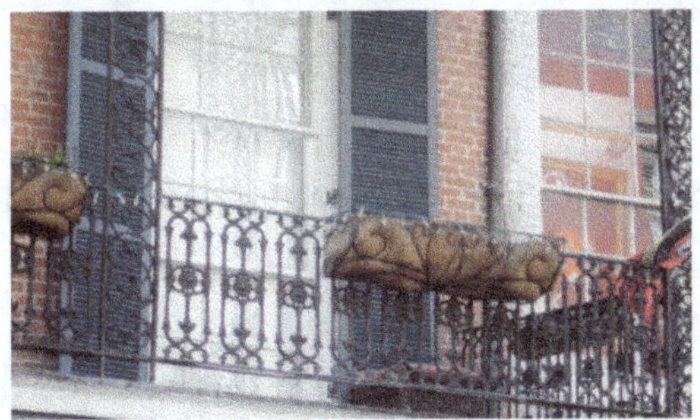

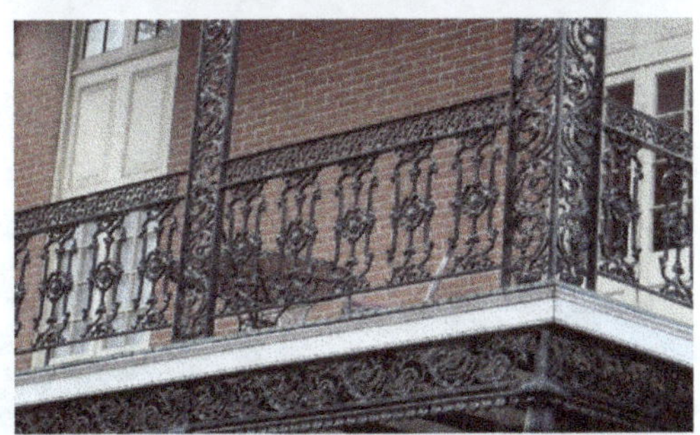
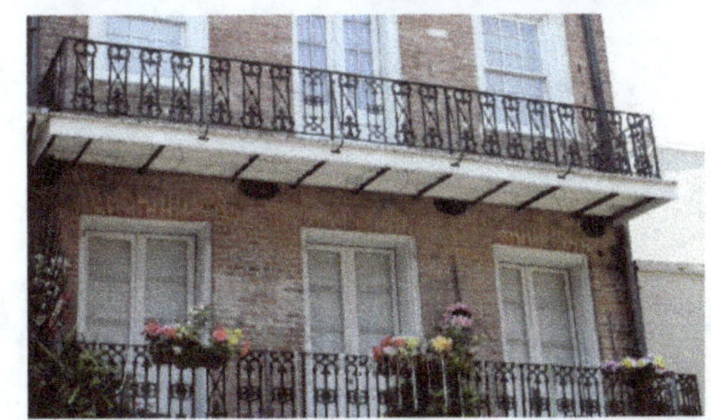

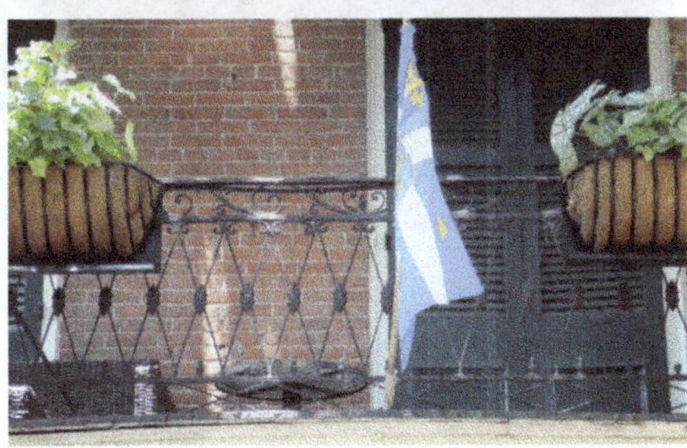
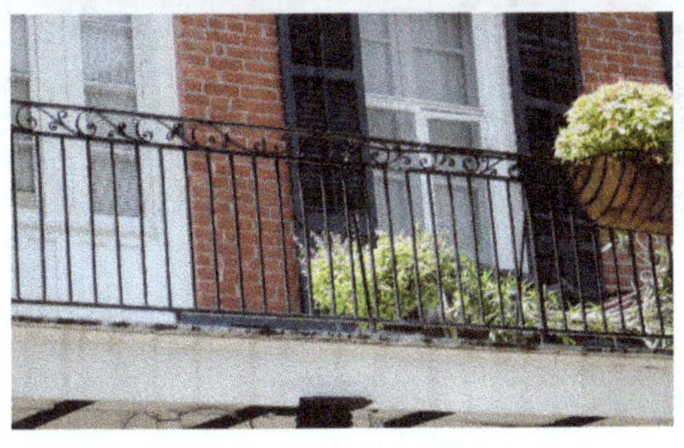

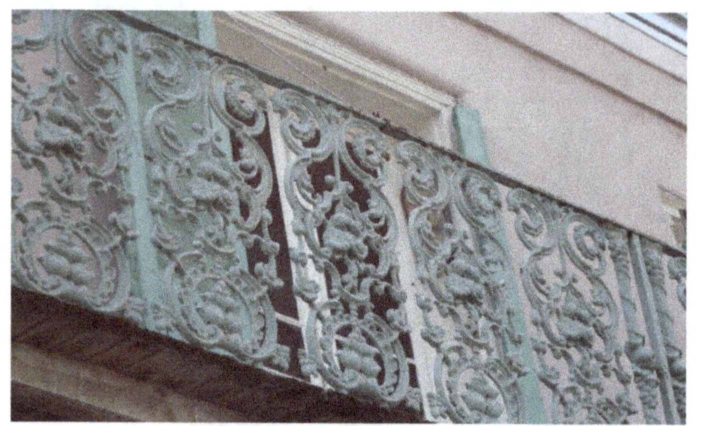

Fleur de Lis and Hearts

While the United States has several places which have wrought ironwork, New Orleans contains more than any other examples found in the country. The concentration of wrought and cast irons lends New Orleans, especially in the French Quarter, or the Vieux Carre, such a unique distinction.

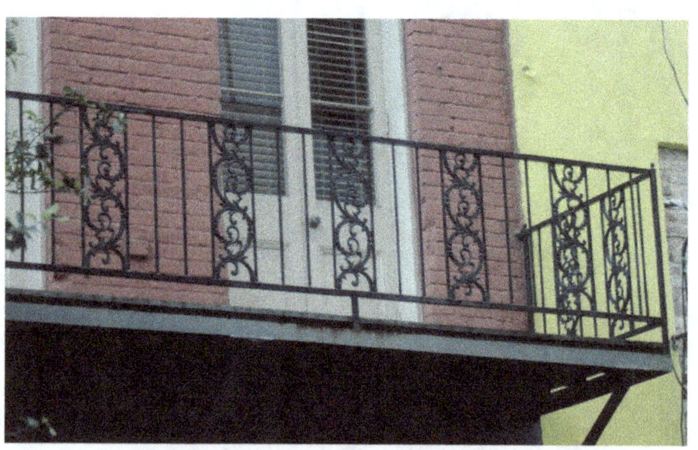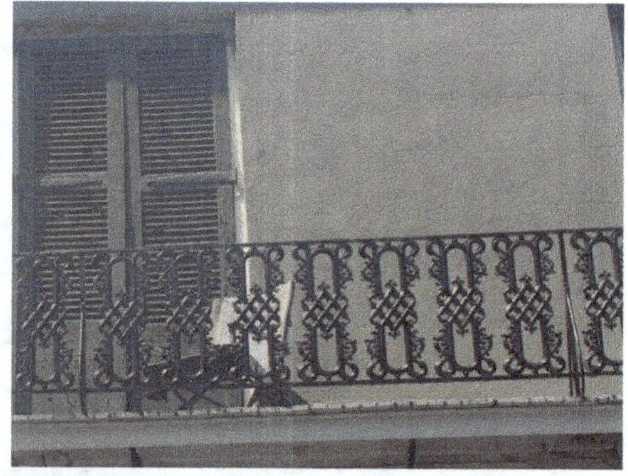

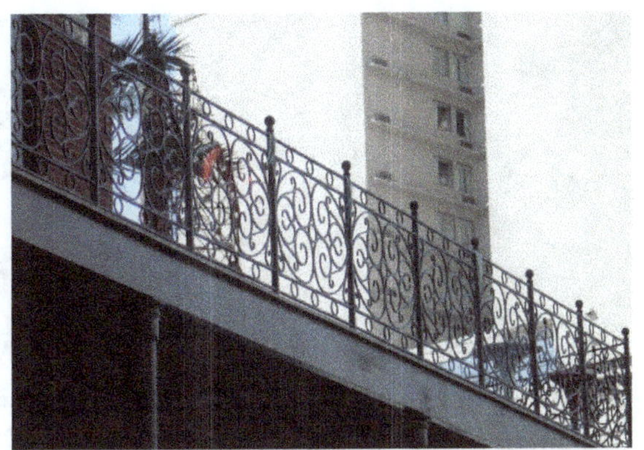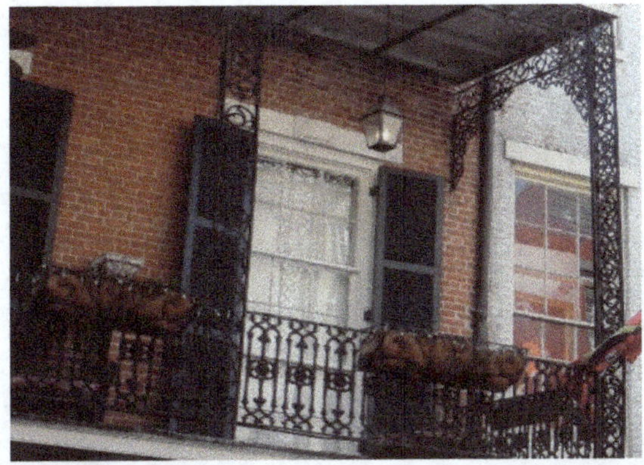

Barcelona style scrollwork

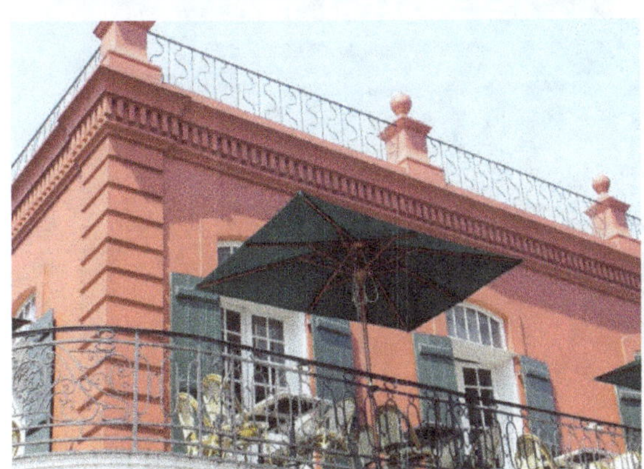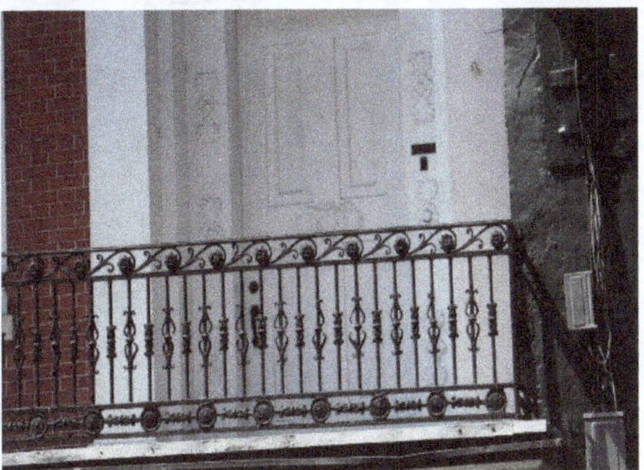

Often times, a combination of designs and techniques can be seen in one piece as noticed on the right picture.

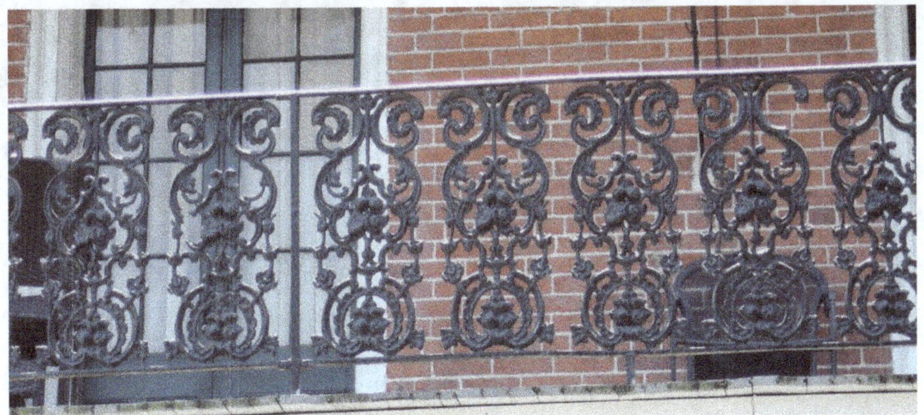

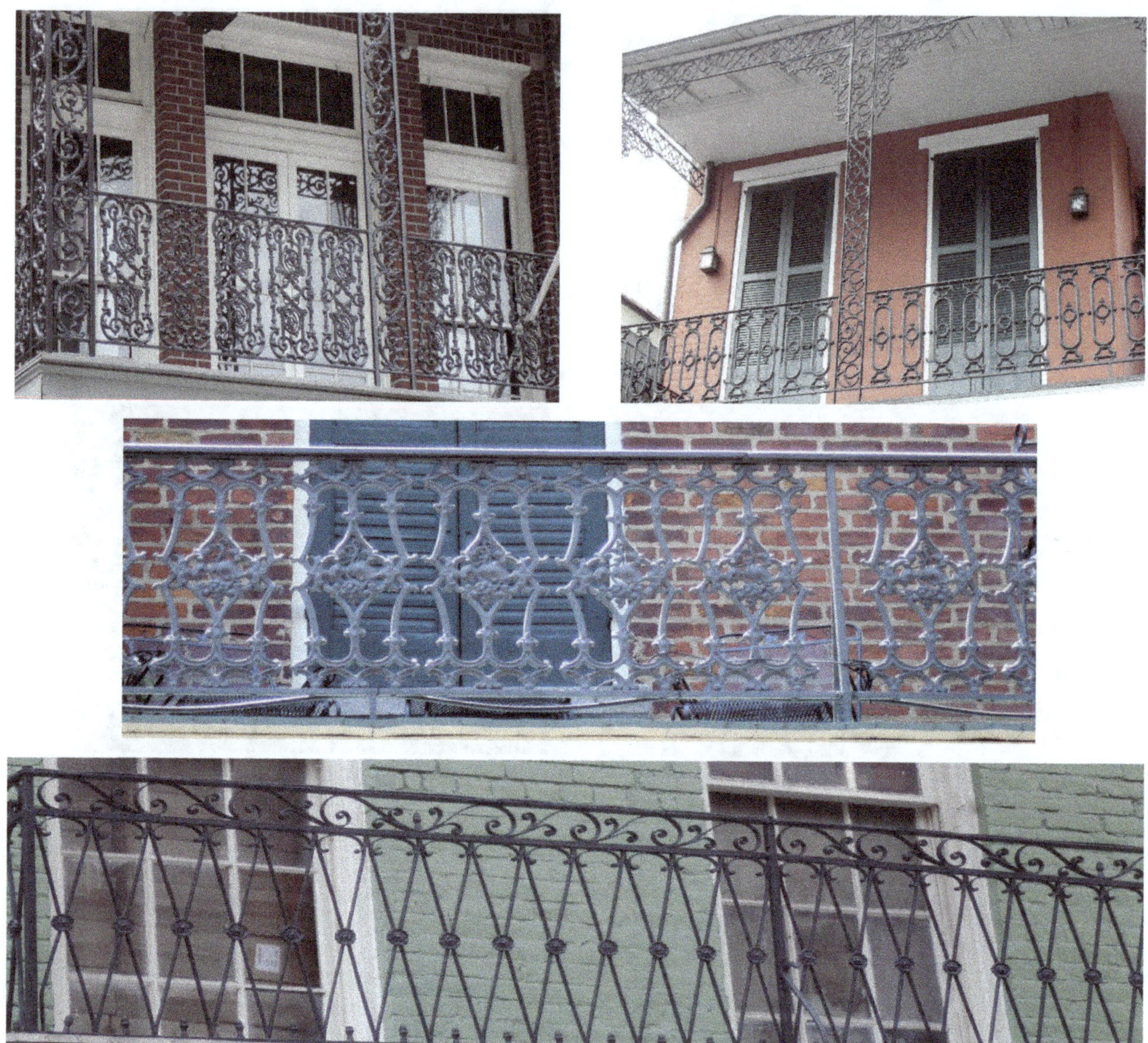

Coen, Lychee Molherbe collars or knots with an open scroll top and a diamond crossbar.

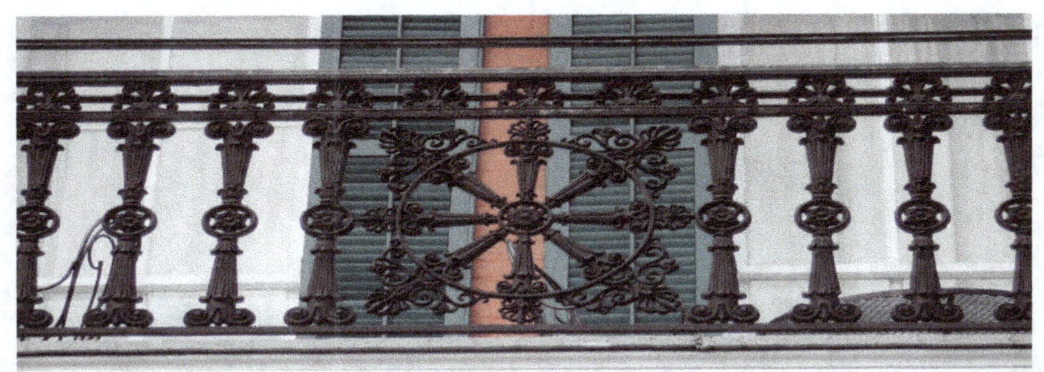

Tulip Casting

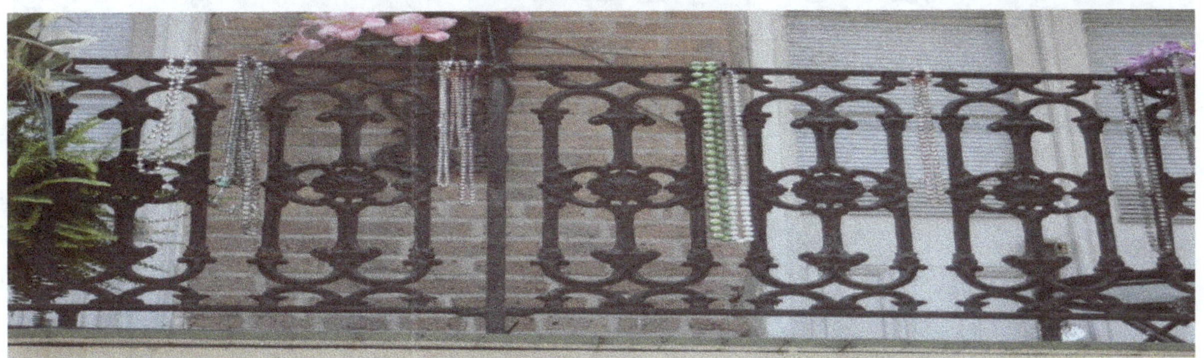

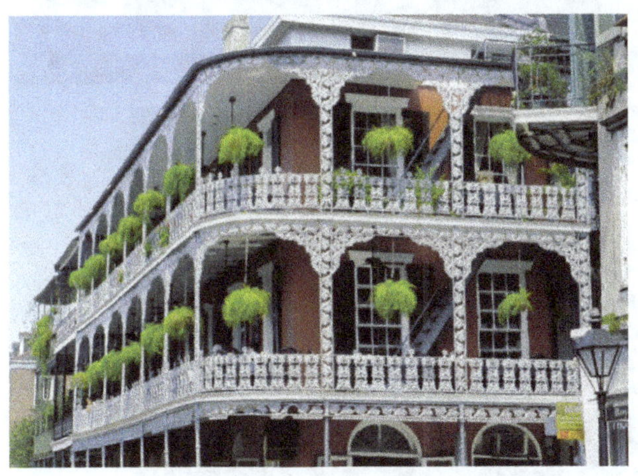

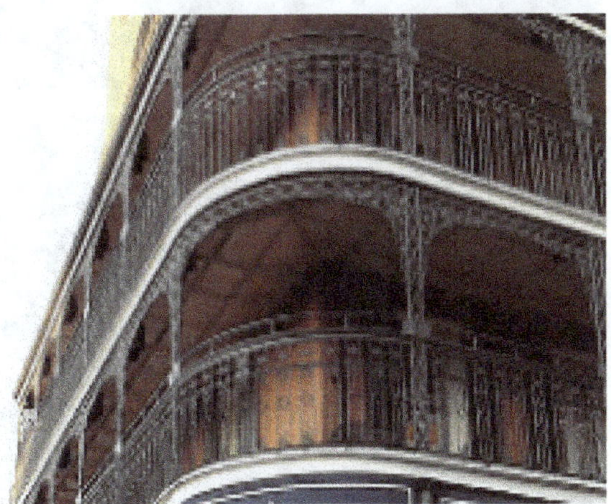

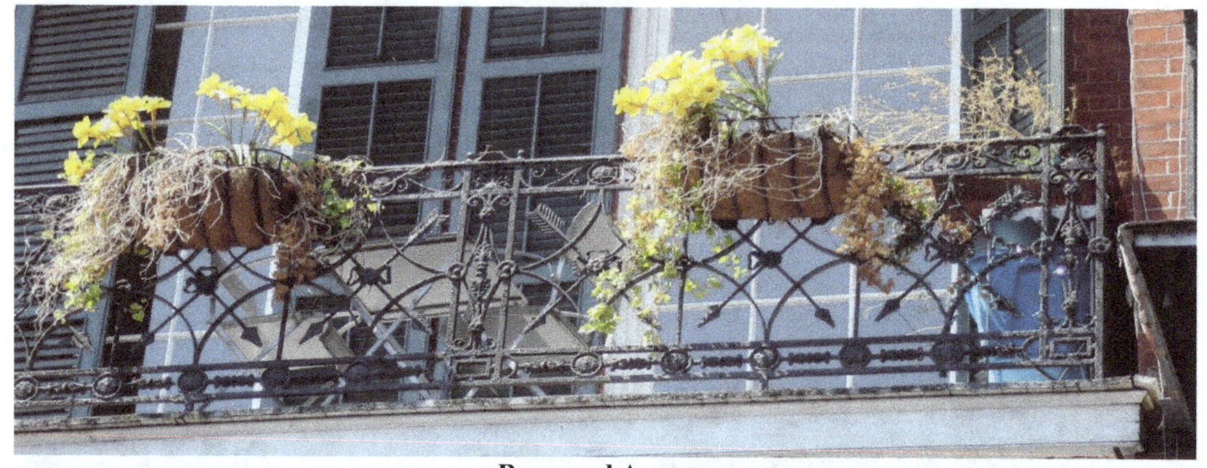

Bows and Arrows

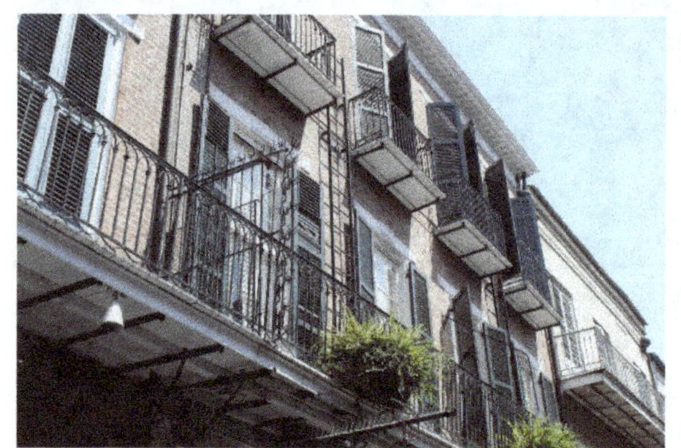

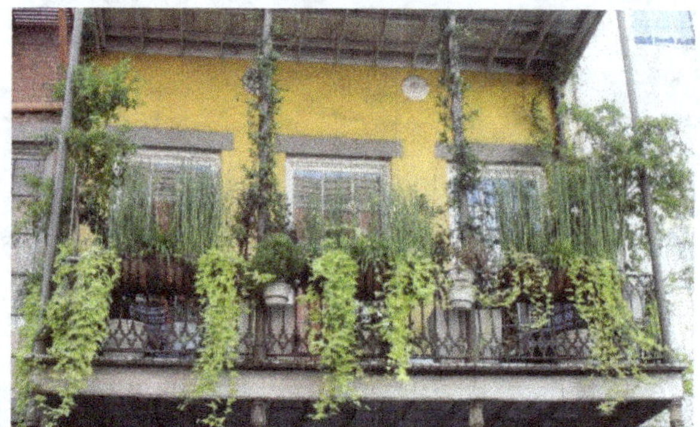

To start the story of New Orleans wrought iron, one must know a bit about the person who hired the blacksmiths to create such everlasting beauty and brought beautification to the city. Micaela Leonarda Antonia Almonester y Rojas, Baroness de Pontalba was born to aristocratic parents in 1795. Her father, Don Andres, was a wealthy Spaniard who gained his fortune while in New Orleans from real estate and land transfers. At the time, New Orleans was part of the Spanish government, even though the inhabitants were predominately of French descent.

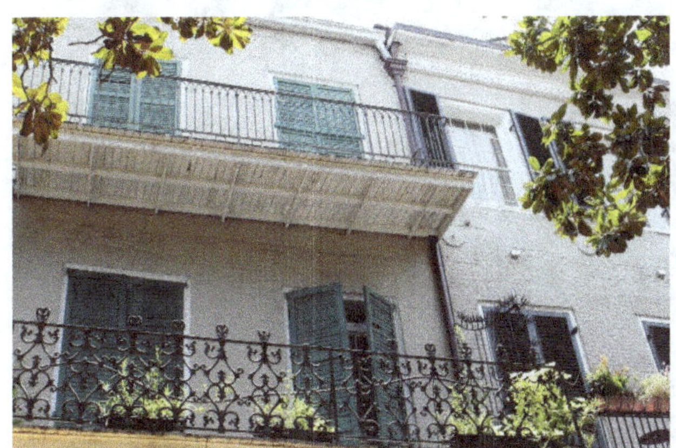

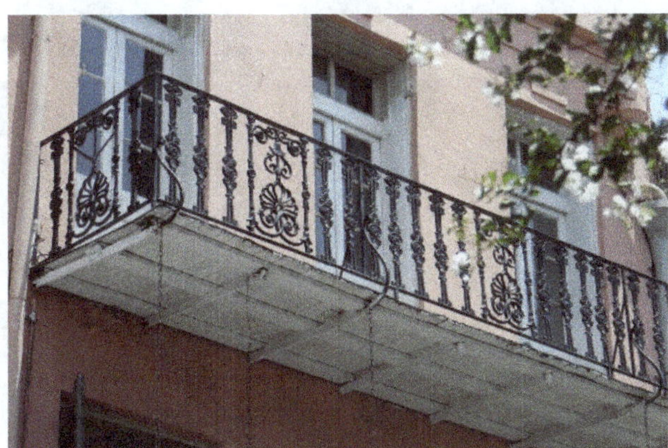

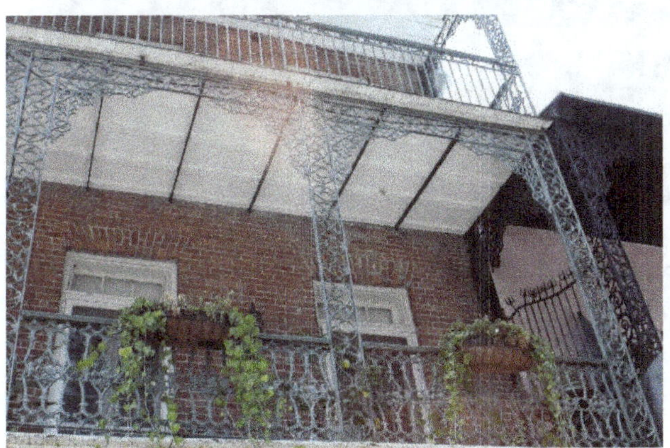

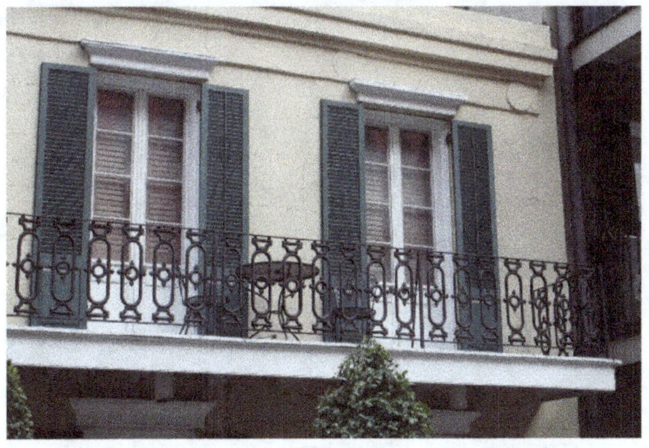

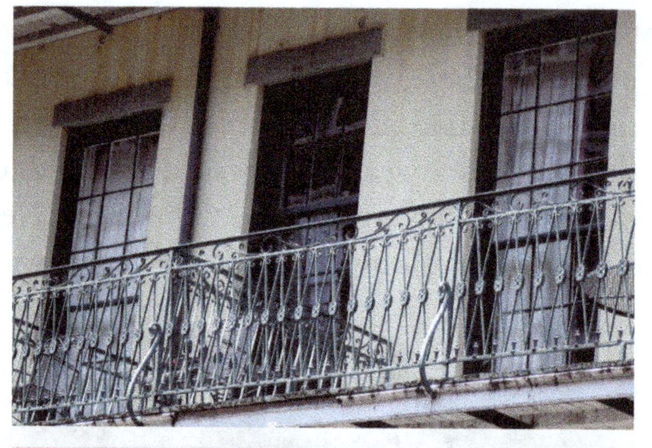
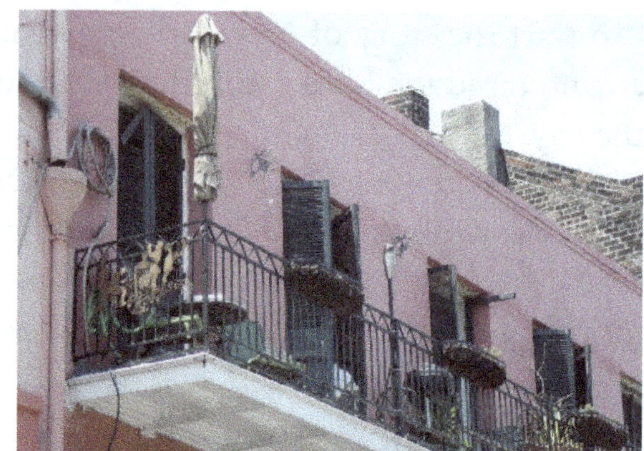
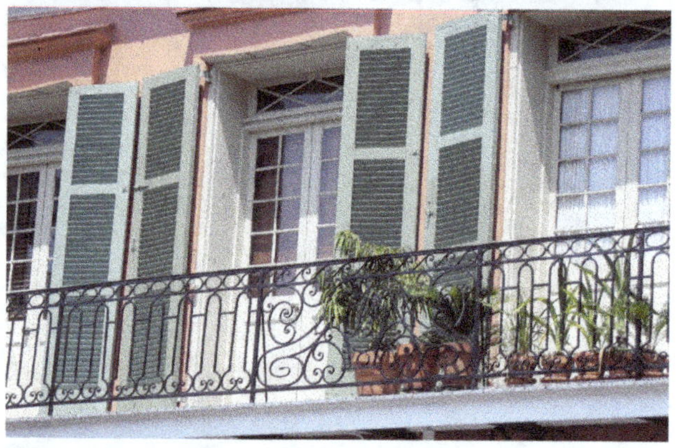
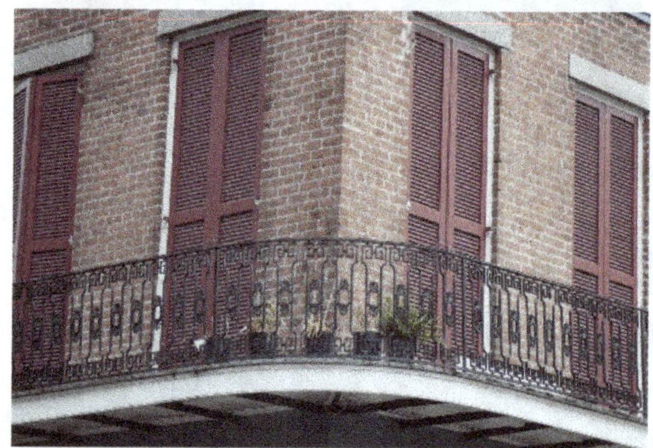
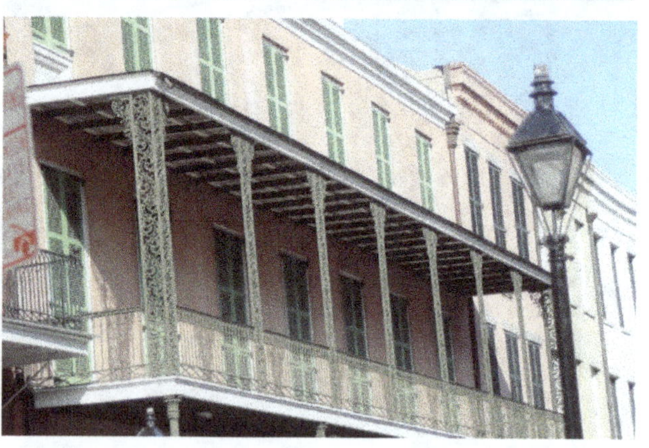
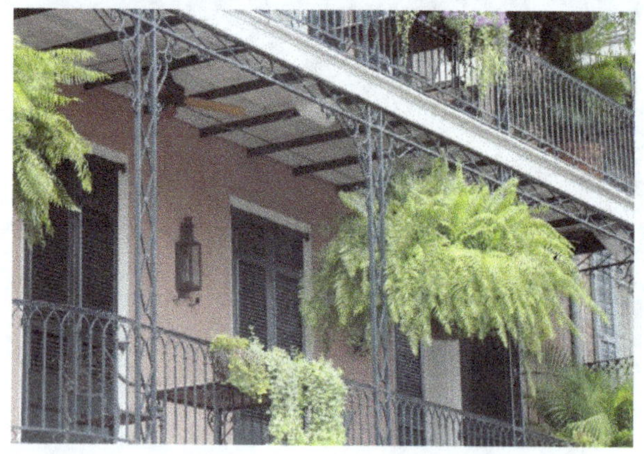

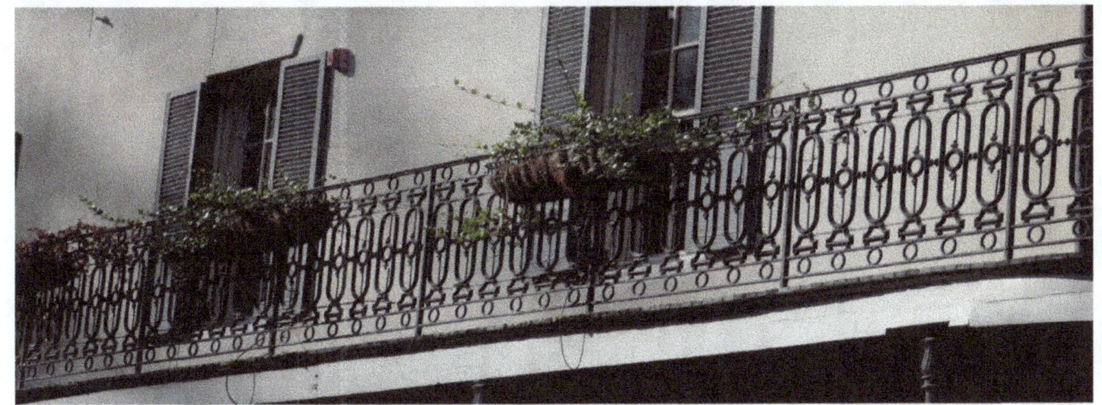

$\mathbf{D}$on married Louise Denis de la Ronde, in 1787, a woman from one of the most illustrious Creole families in Louisiana. Before Don passed away when Micaela was but two and a half years of age, he had commissioned the construction of the St. Louis Cathedral, the Cabildo and Presbytere, which were all located on one side of the Place d'Armes.

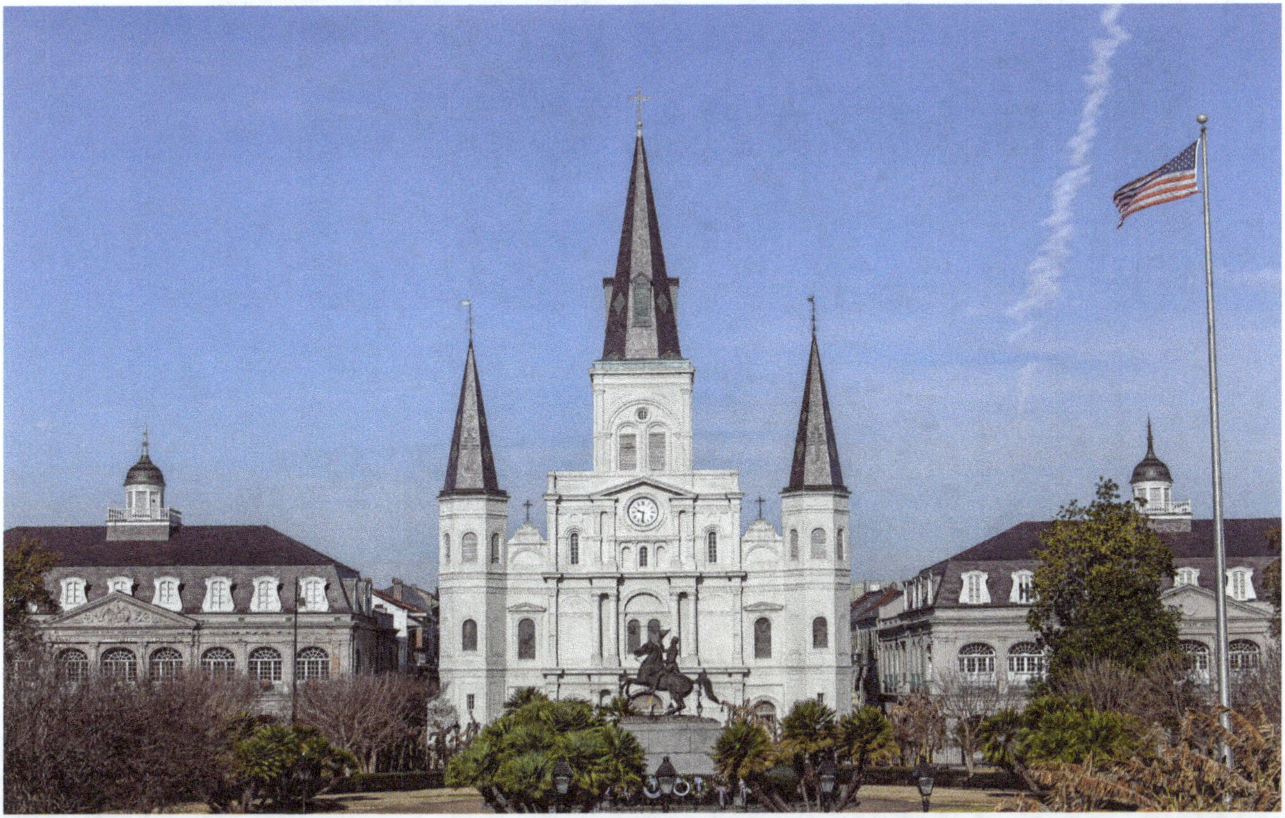

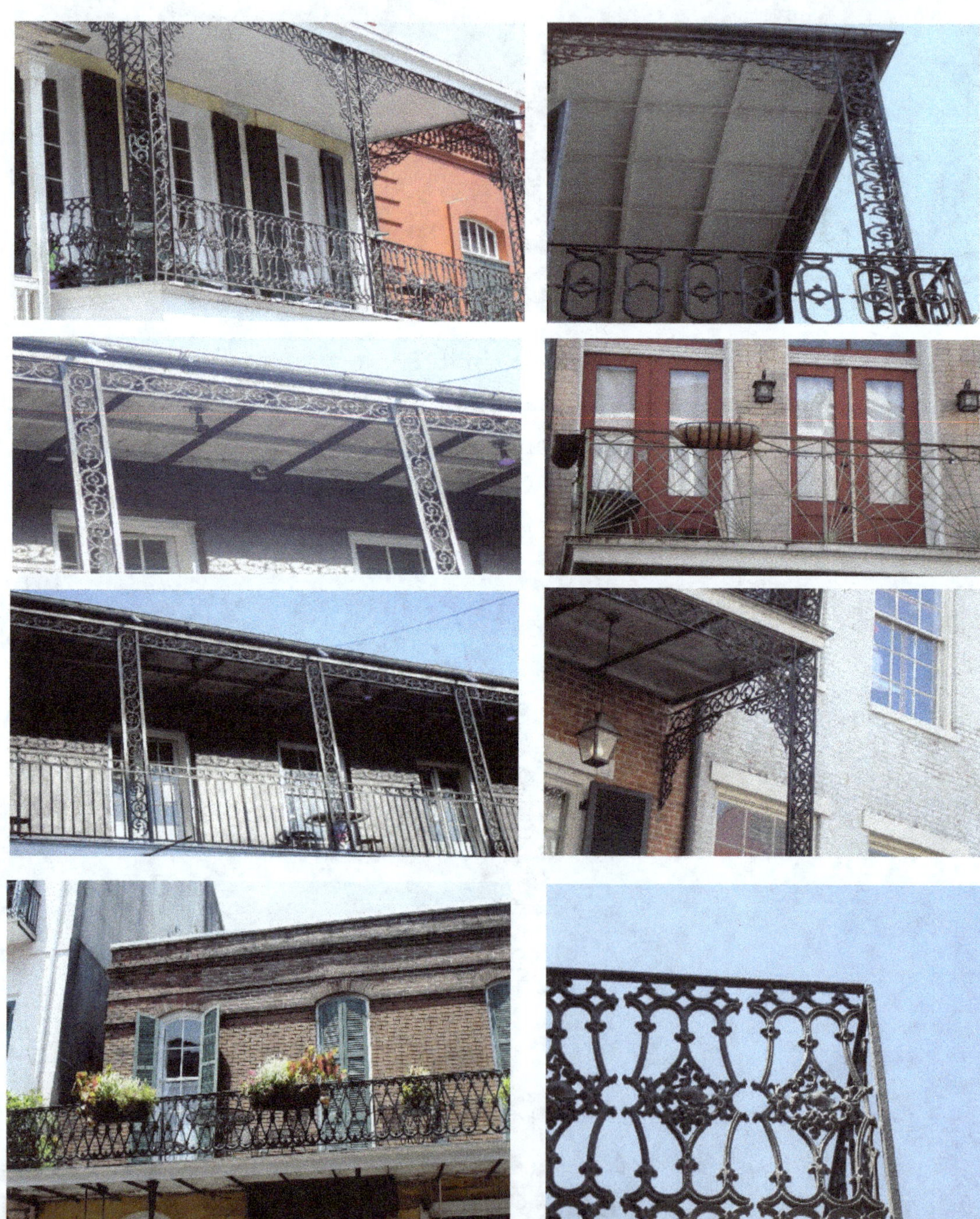

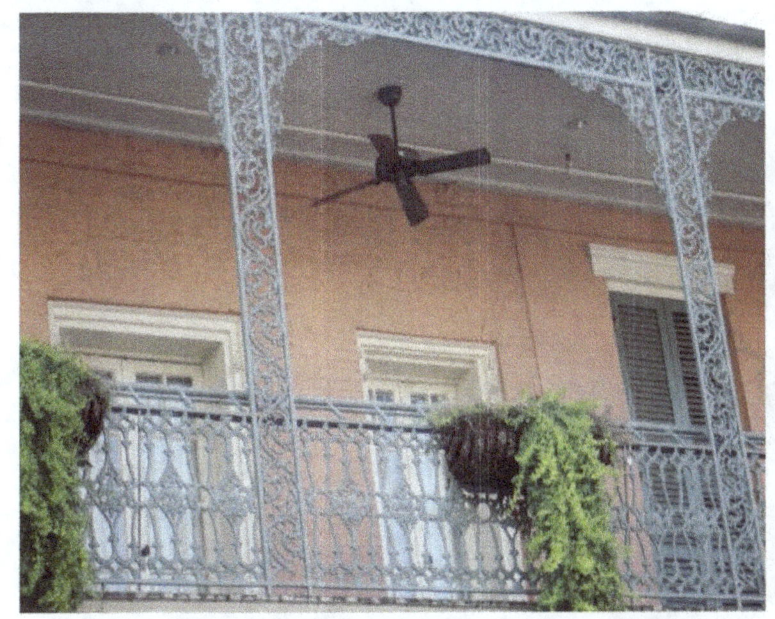
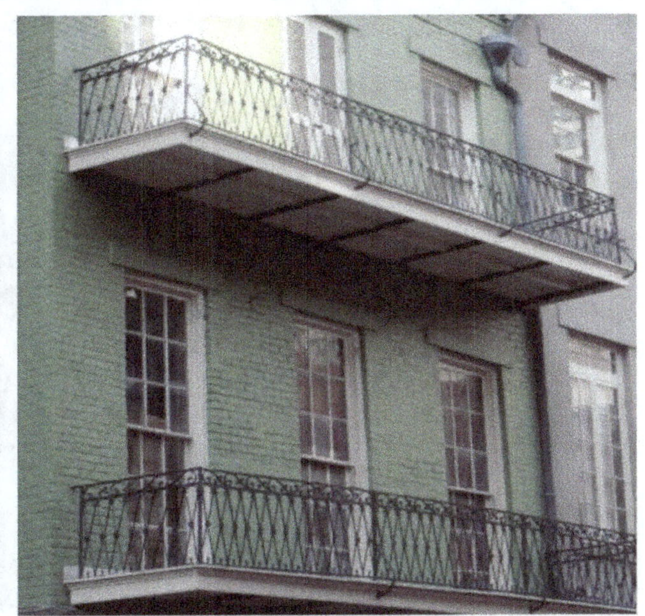
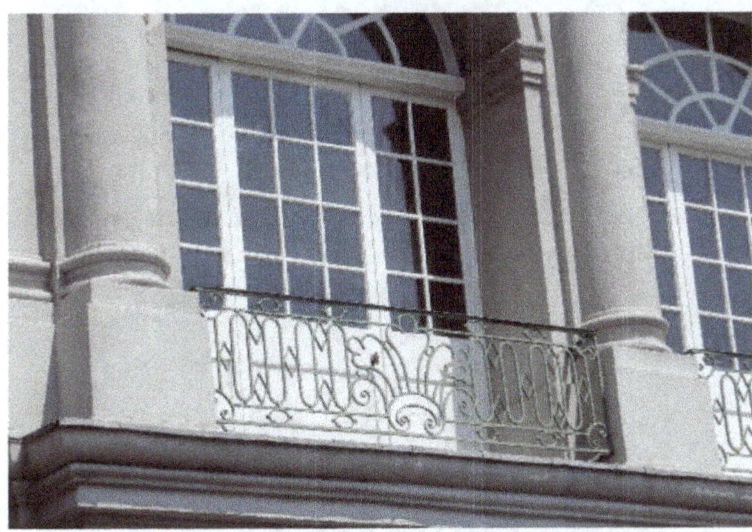
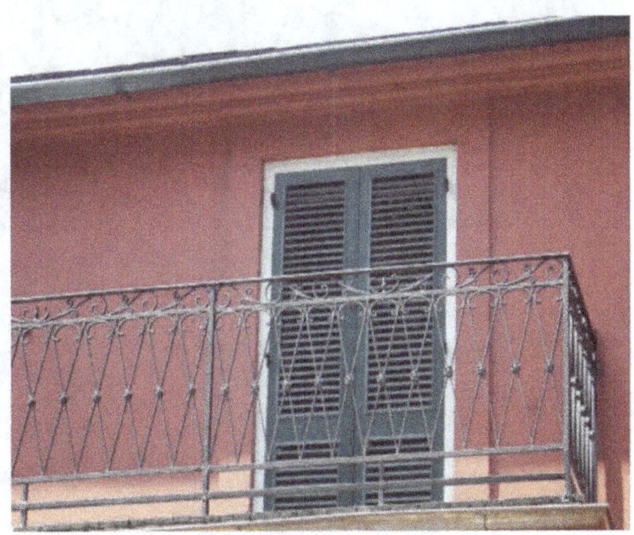

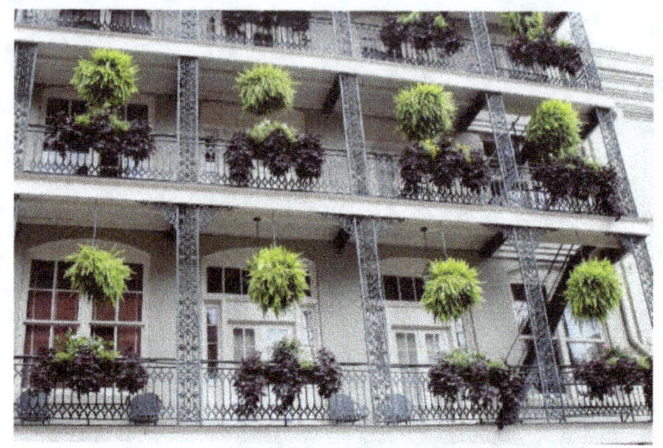
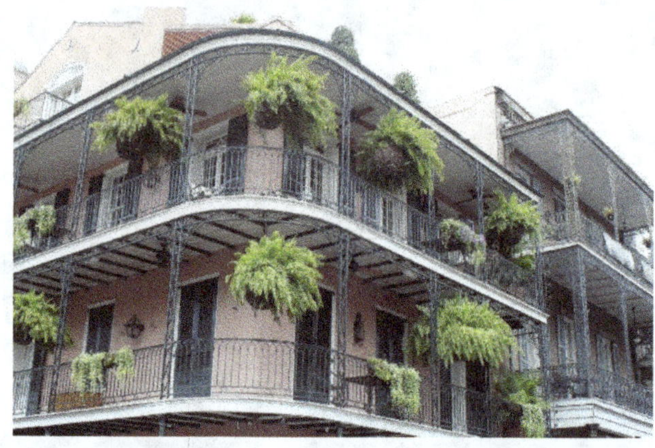
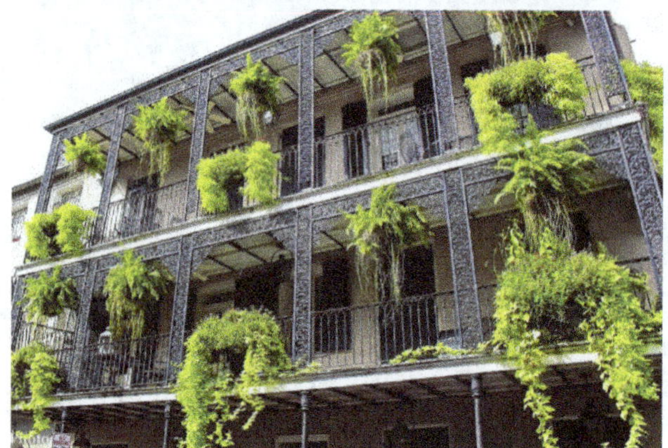
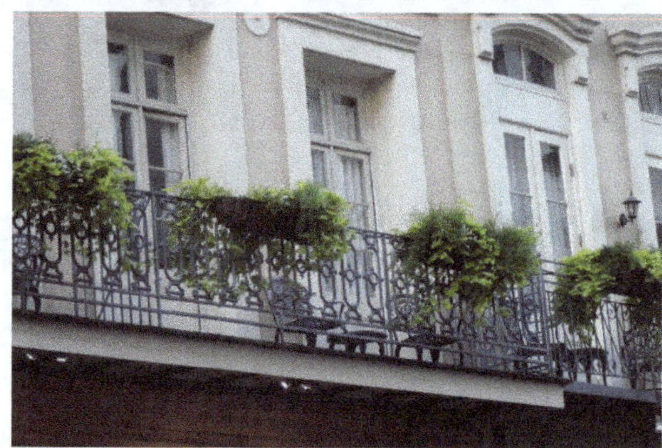
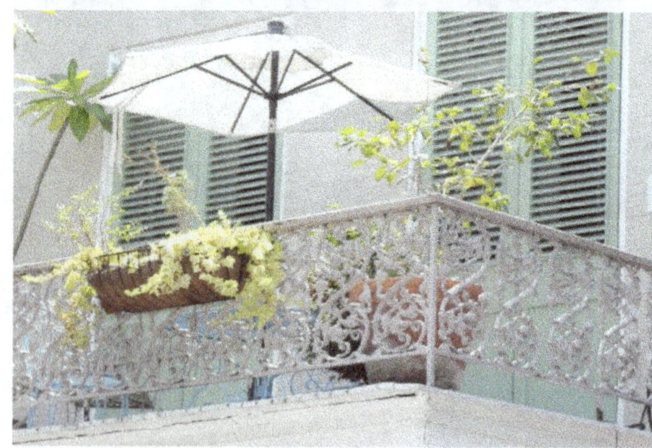
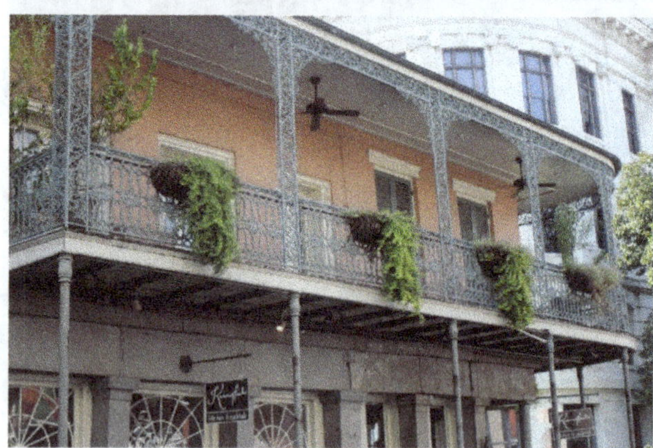

As was tradition in eighteenth and nineteenth centuries, an arranged marriage for Micaela to her cousin, Xavier Célestin Delfau de Pontalba, occurred in 1811, when she was only 15, despite the fact she was in love with someone else. It's been stated her husband's father was displeased with Micaela and the amount of money she had in her dowry, even though that was the agreed upon amount. After her mother's death, her father-in-law, Baron Joseph Delfau de Pontalba became so greedy and jealous, of Micaela's private wealth, he took a dueling pistol and shot Micaela four times in the chest before turning the pistol upon himself.

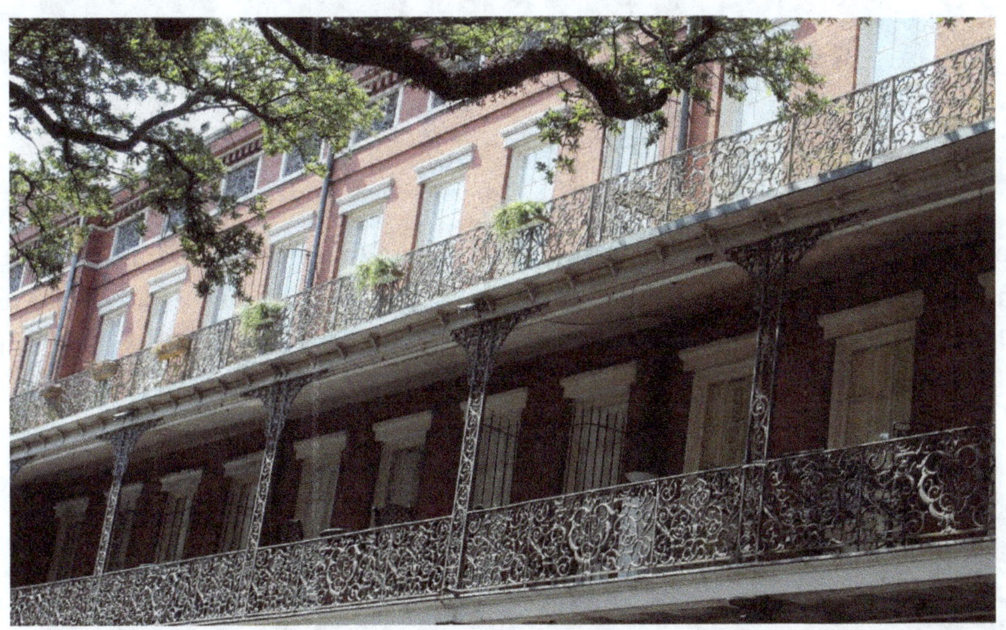

Despite the point blank range of the shots, Micaela survived the attack and returned to New Orleans from her previous residence in France. When she returned to New Orleans, she found the city in disrepair. Using her own money from her inheritance, she began repairing and building to help beautify the city. Among the many endeavors she undertook were the construction of the Pontalba Apartments, red bricked structures which flanked either side of the Cathedral, Cabildo and Presbytere. The ironwork which decorated the balconies were also of her design and included her initials AP in each section.

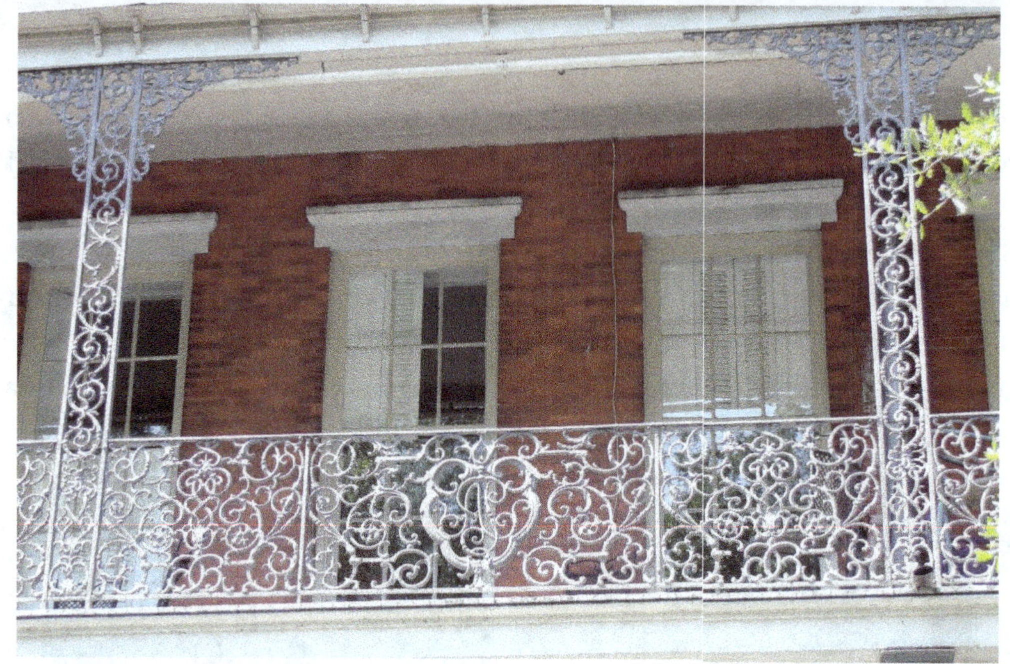

Micaela was also instrumental in changing the Place d'Armes from a parade ground to that of a formal garden, which would also include a statue of Andrew Jackson, hero of the Battle of New Orleans. She met Jackson years before while he was President of the United States. This was just one of her many beautification projects.

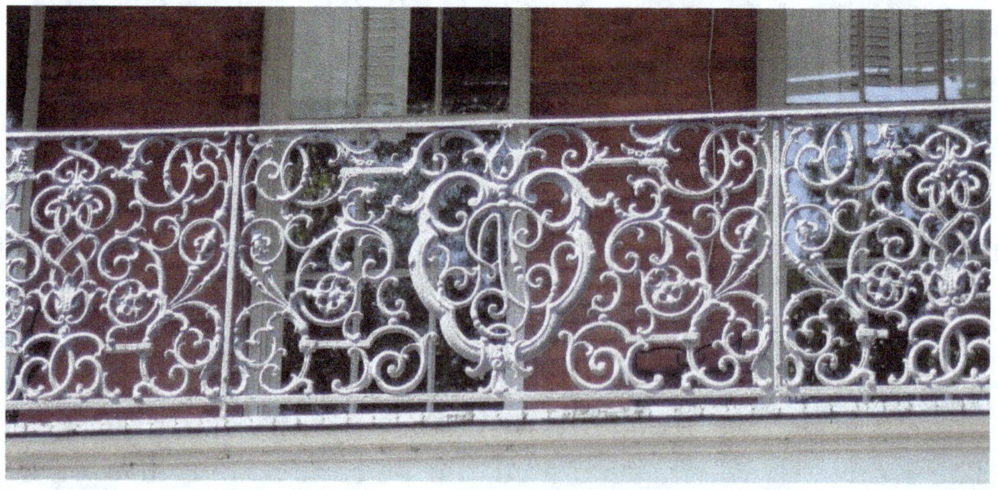

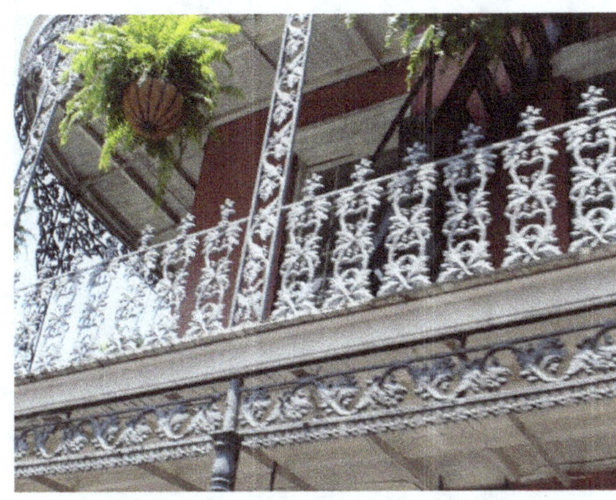

Oak Casting

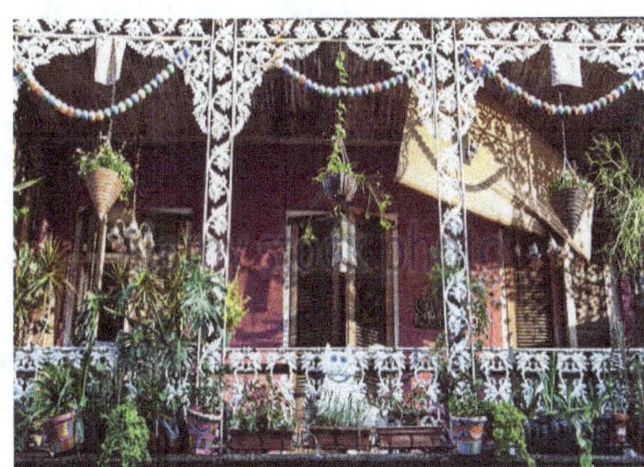

Grape casting decorated with beads.

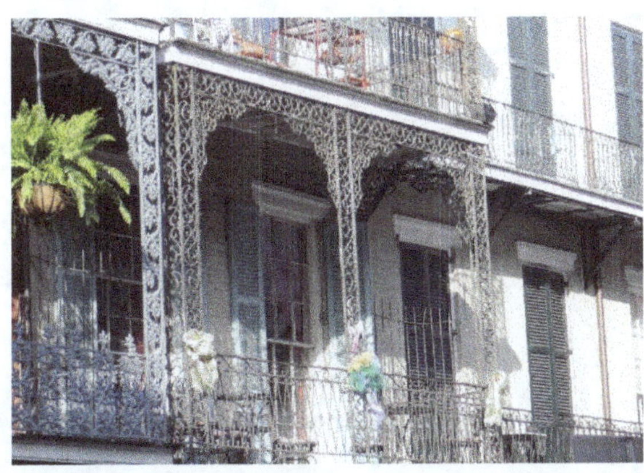

Bellflower casting

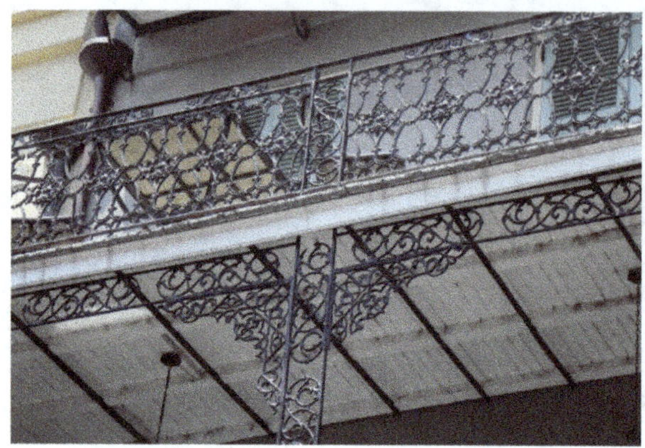

Mixed Motif's incluidng Open C, Scroll S and grapes.

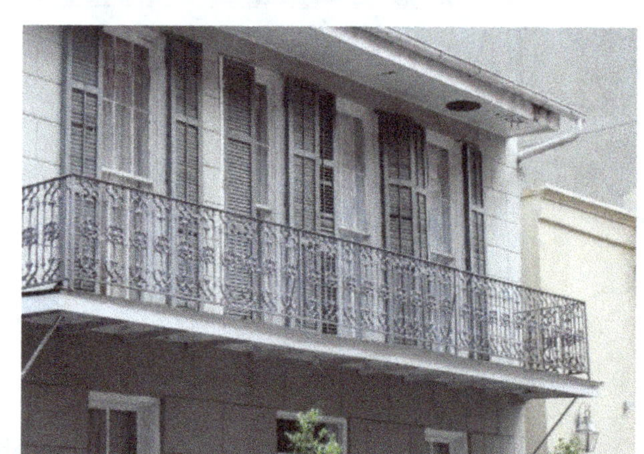

Double arches with clam shells.

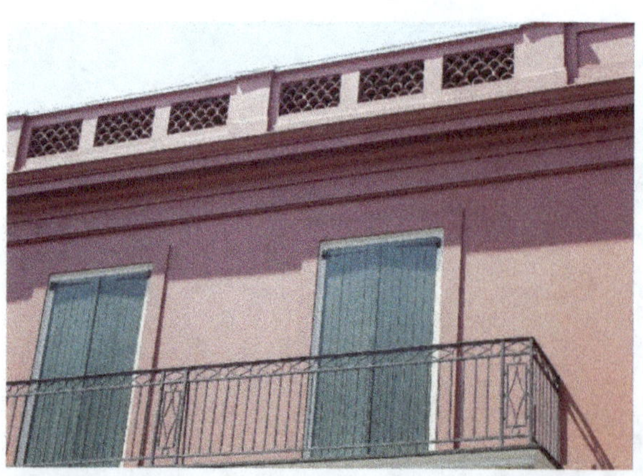

Simple bar with diamond braces and scallop vents

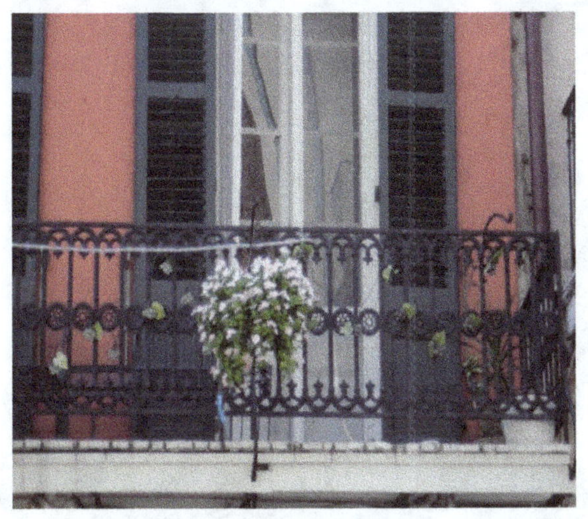
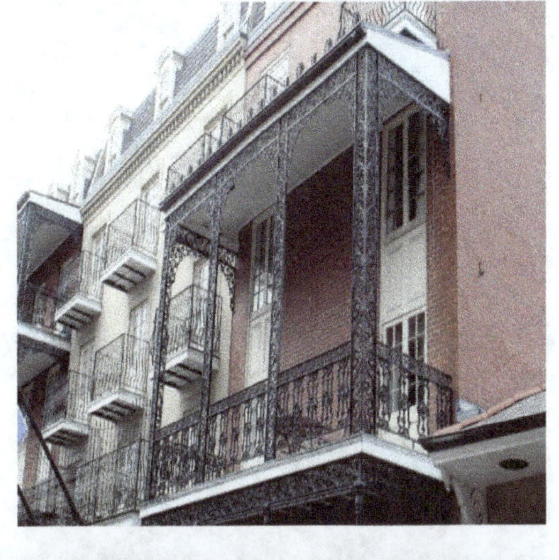
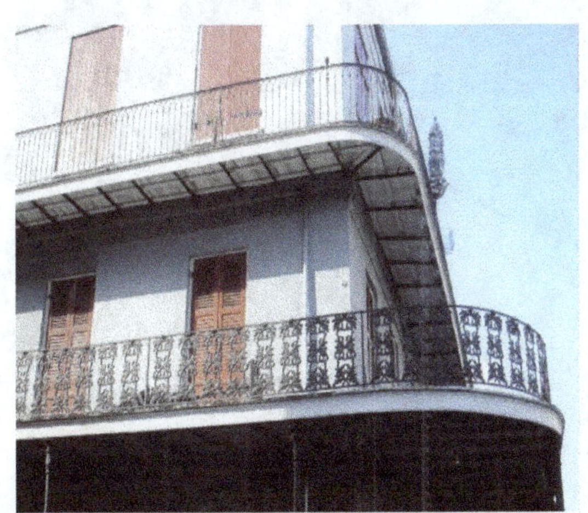
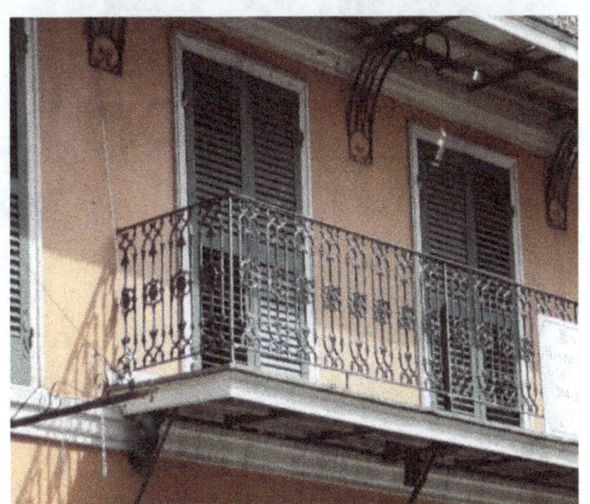
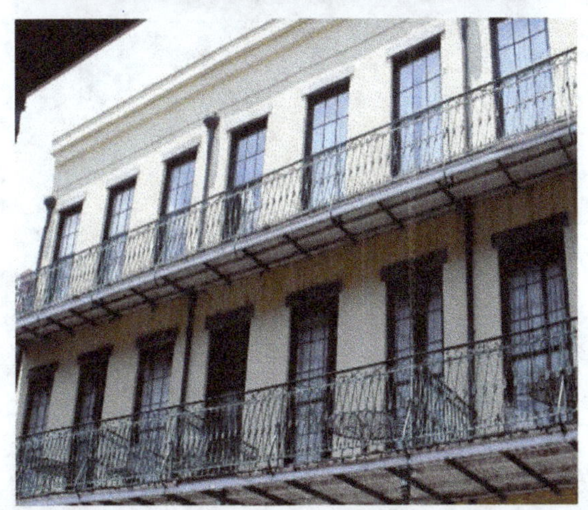
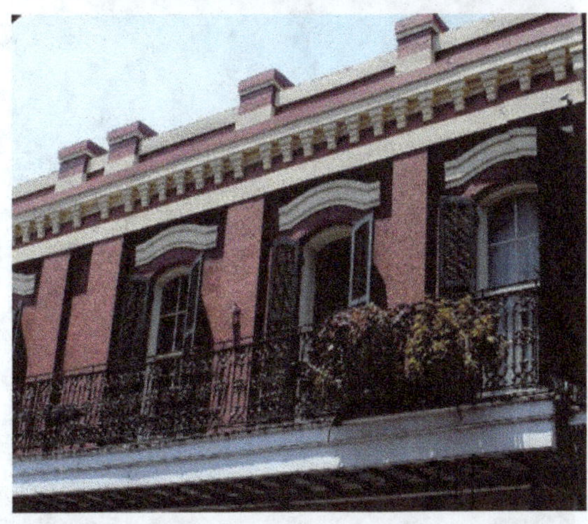

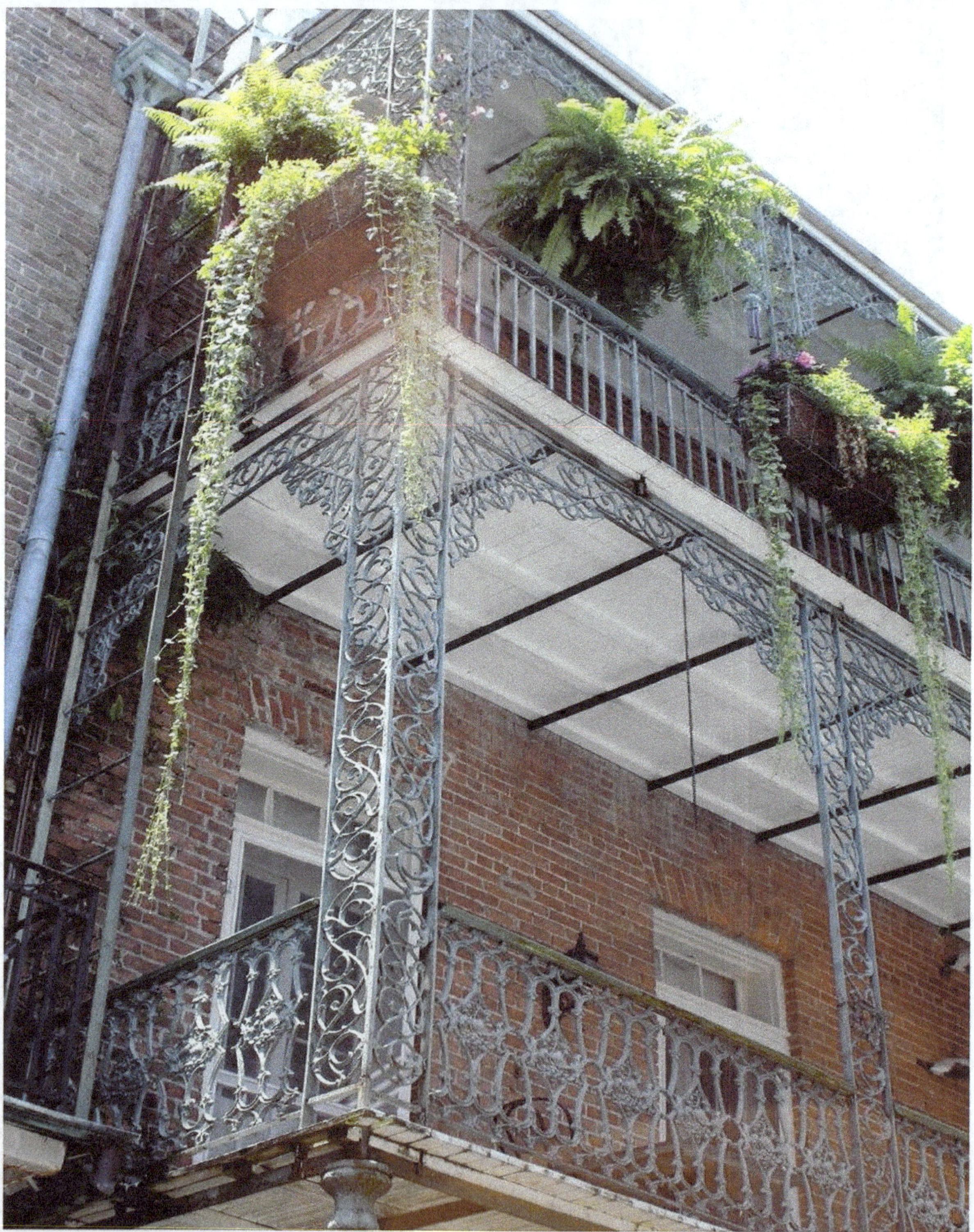

New Orleans inhabitants encouraged spear like fences and Devil's pitchforks for barriers to entering another's property, whether it be balcony enclosures or climbing over a fence, these pointy pieces of ironwork served as a determent to those who might otherwise trespass.

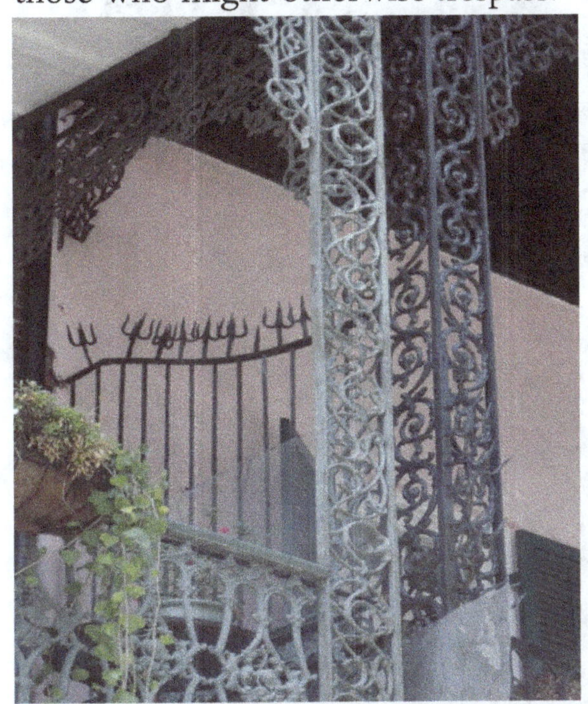

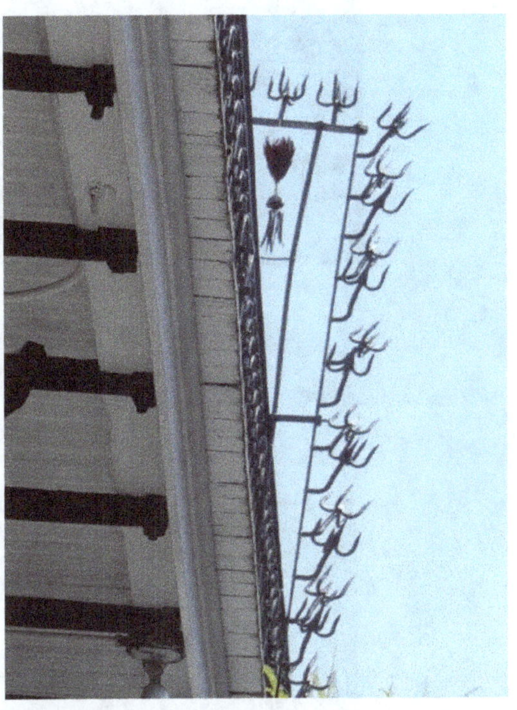

Greek Key motif and Poseidon's Trident also called a Devil's Pitchfork.

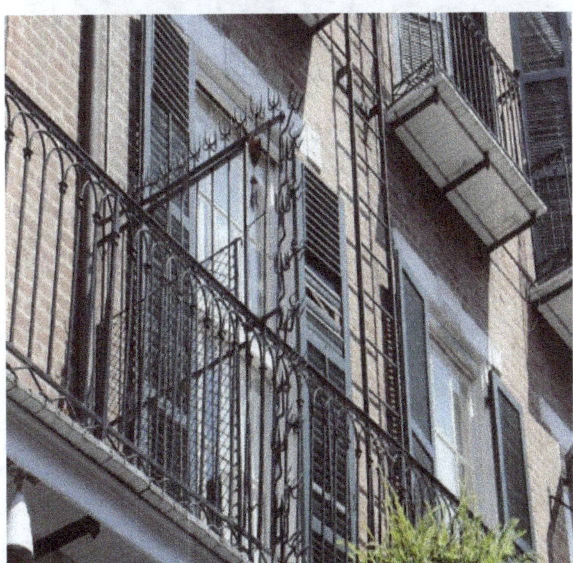

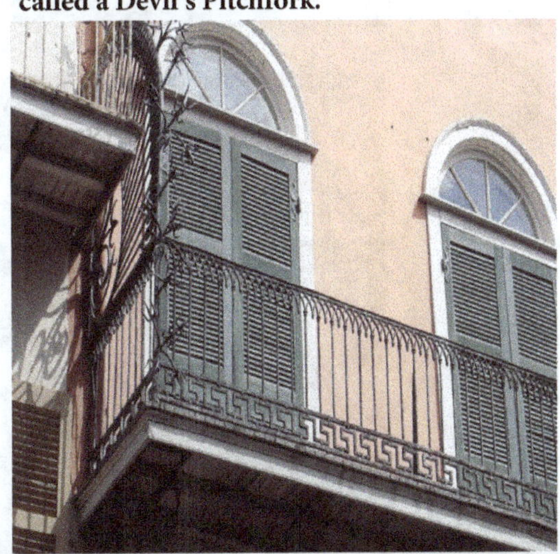

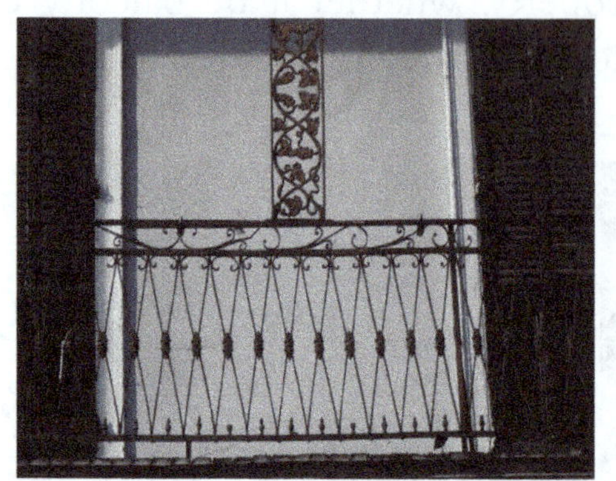
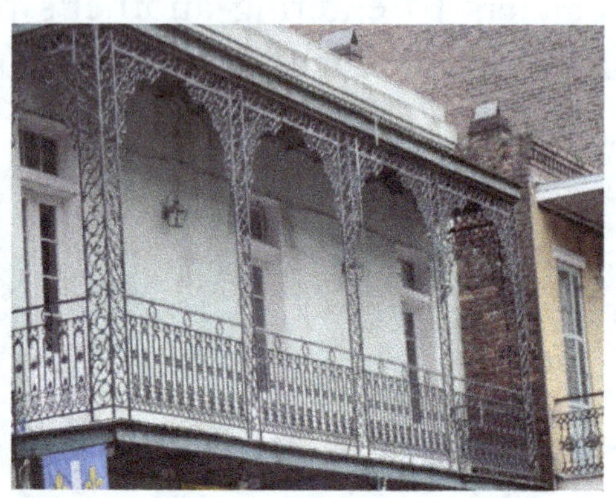
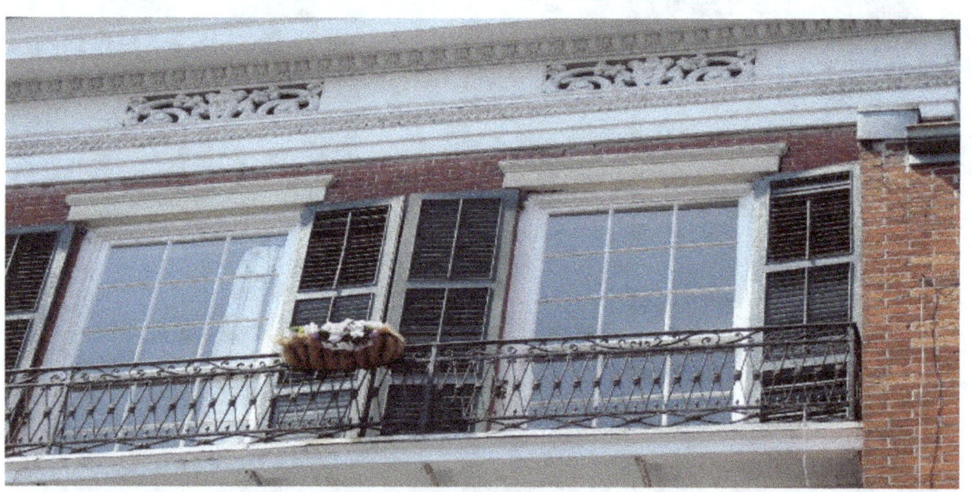
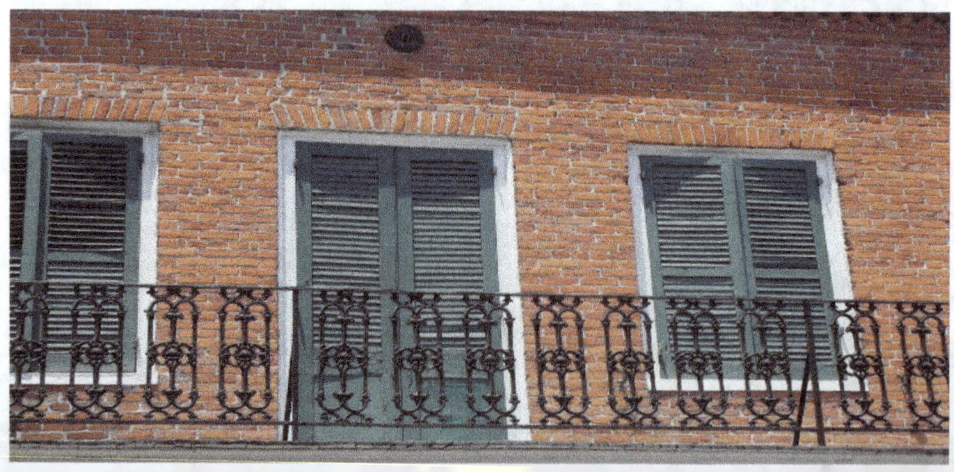

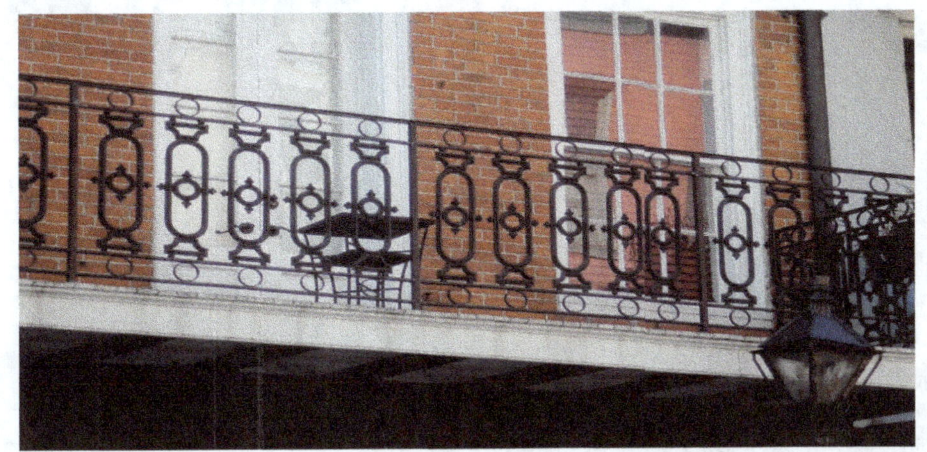

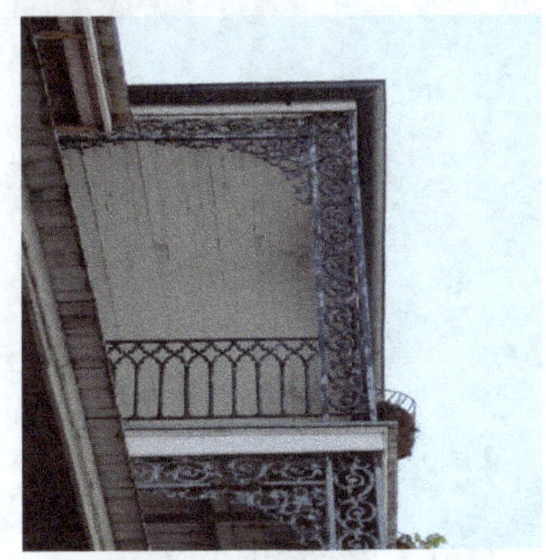

Most of the ironwork created since the early 1800's and brought in extensively after 1850 was done by blacksmith slaves and black freemen. Creoles were also a major contributor to the elaborate detail work of creating wrought iron. Creoles are a mixture of French or Spanish descent who married Louisiana locals, and is originally a French word to distinguish those born in Louisiana as opposed to those born in the mother country.

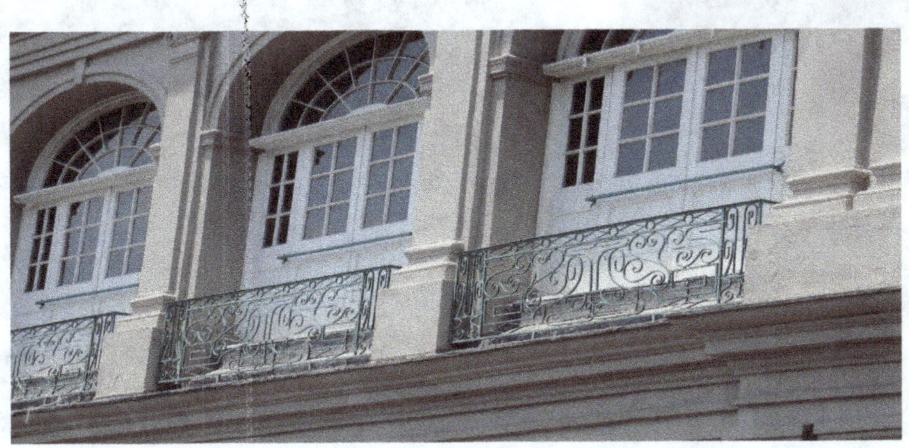

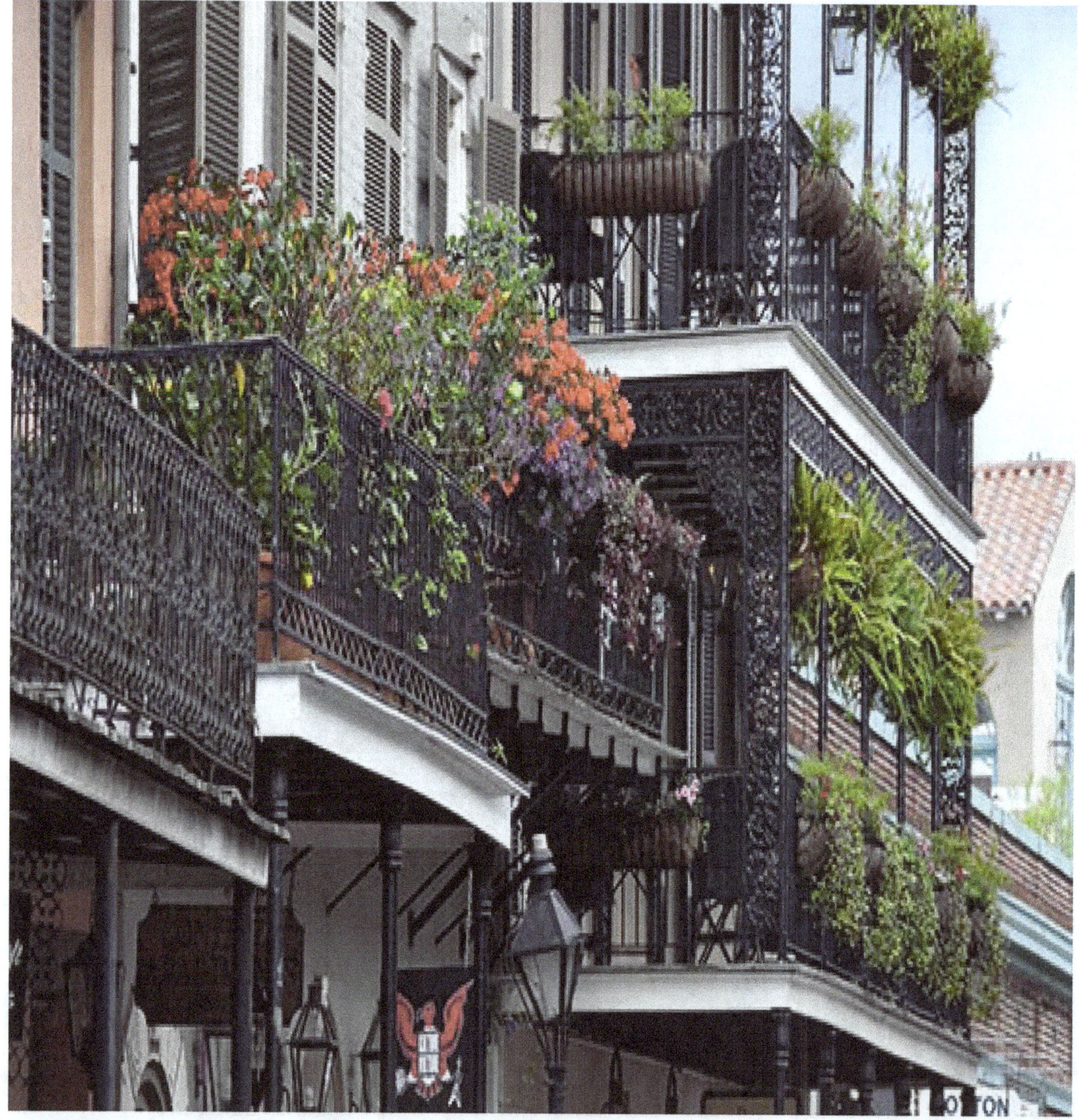
OTTON

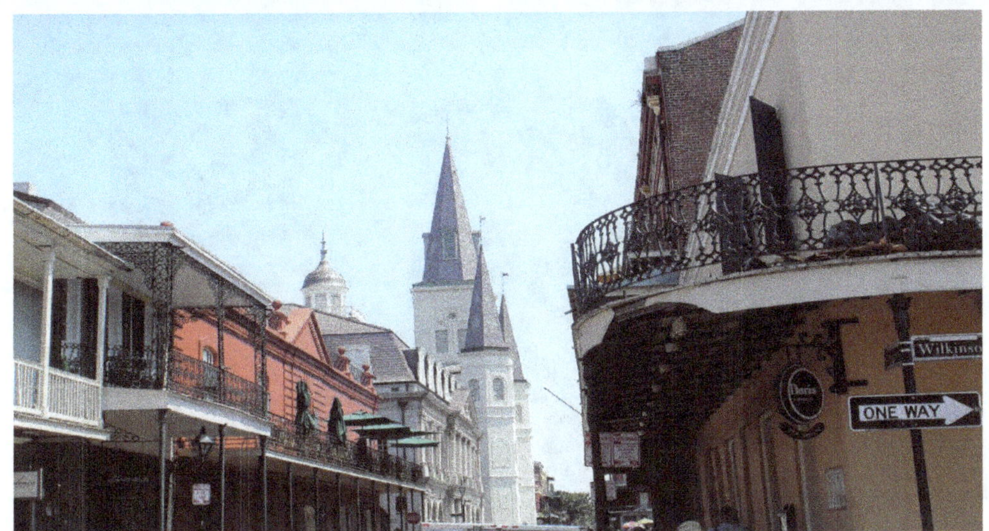

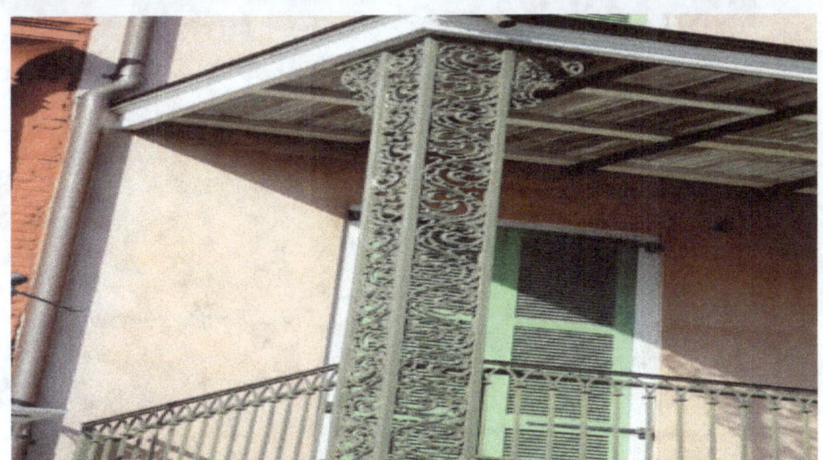

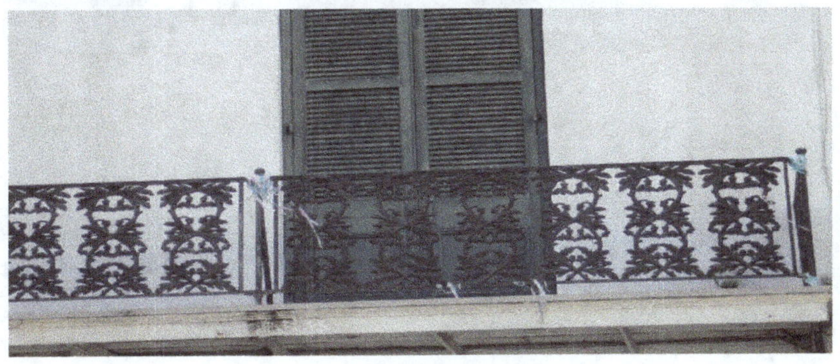

Ivy Leaf Motif

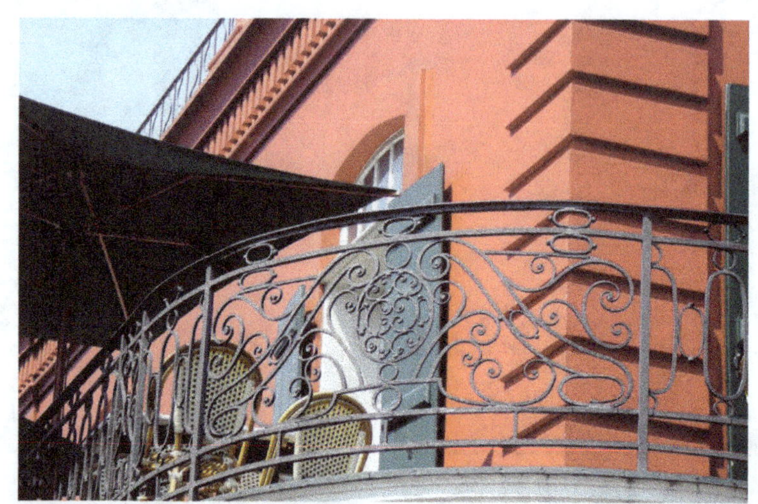

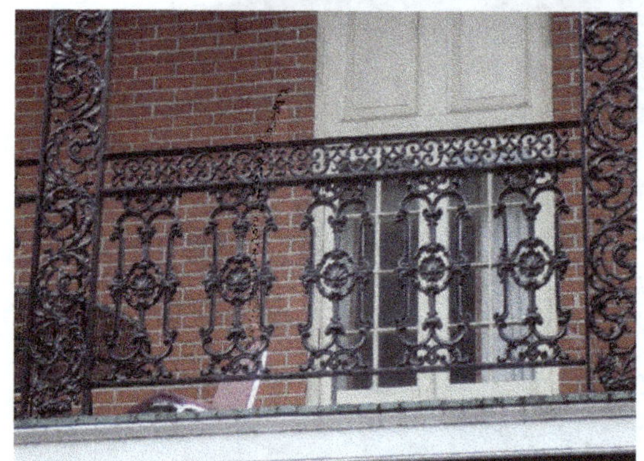

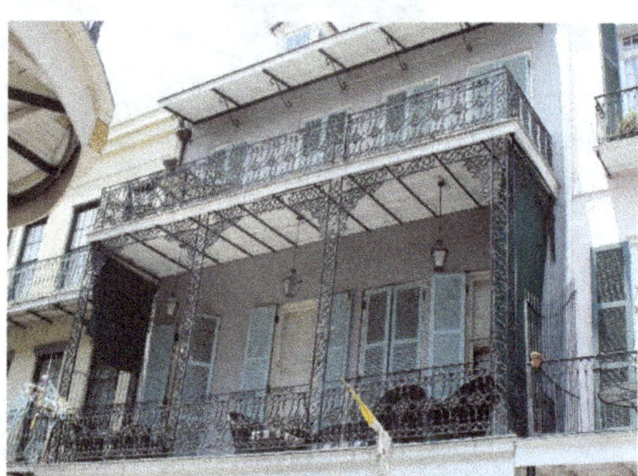

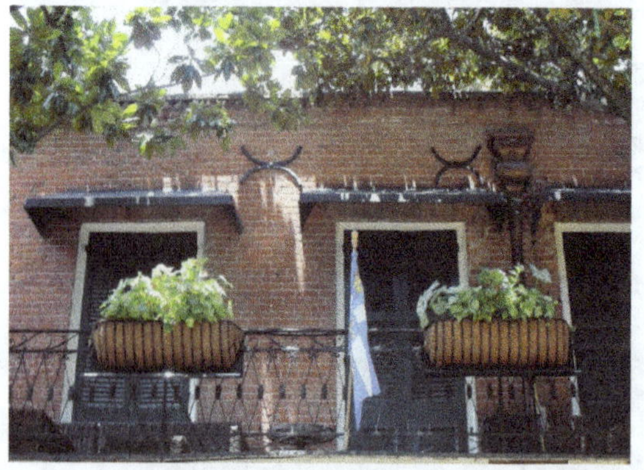

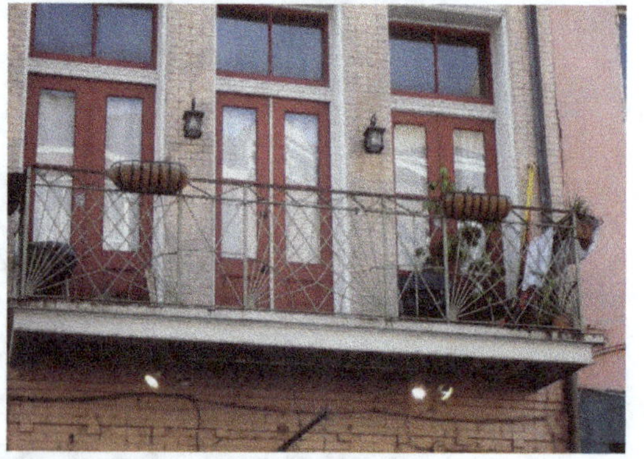

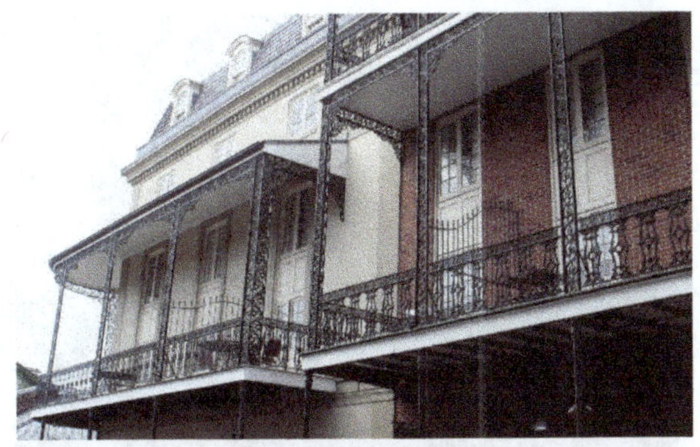
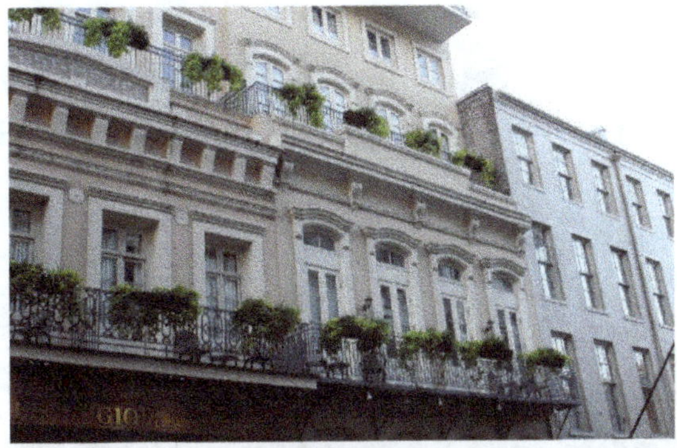
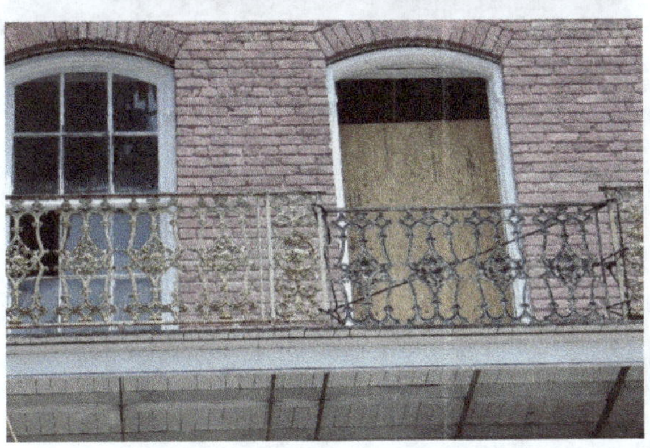
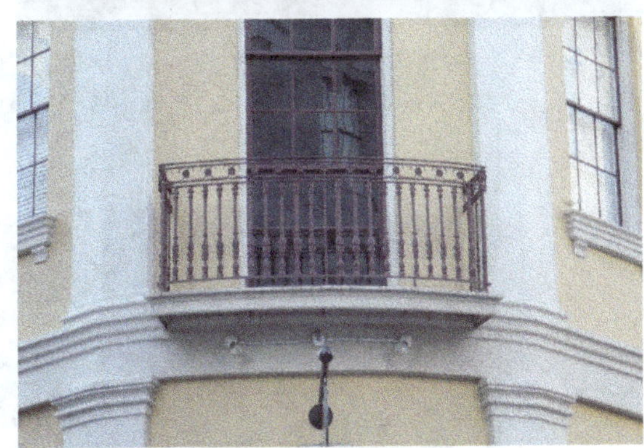

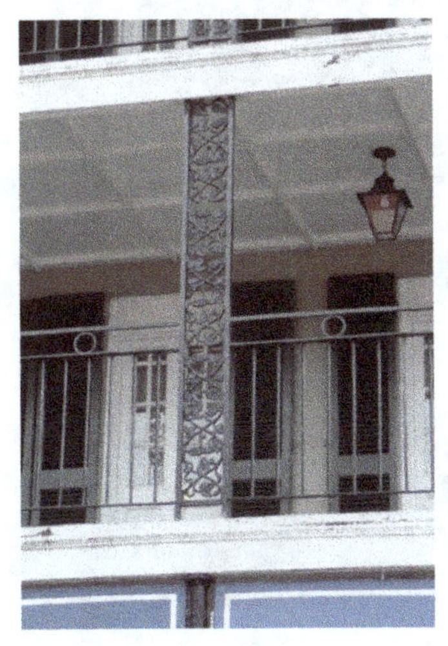

The work done by the blacksmiths of the era created an everlasting moment in time which has been captured and preserved for all to enjoy. The essence of what makes New Orleans French Quarter so unique to any and all who visit stand as a testament to the ability and artistic creativity. of those in the 1700 and 1800's. These iron worker artists, displayed their handiwork and designs openly, which endured a multitude of decades and will continue to delight those who have yet to come and experience the city for themselves.

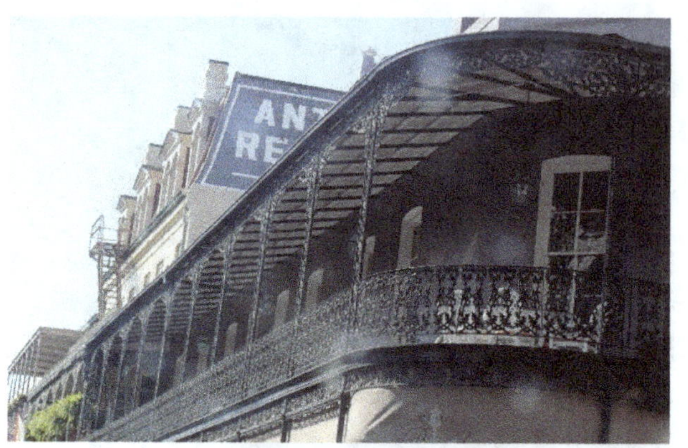
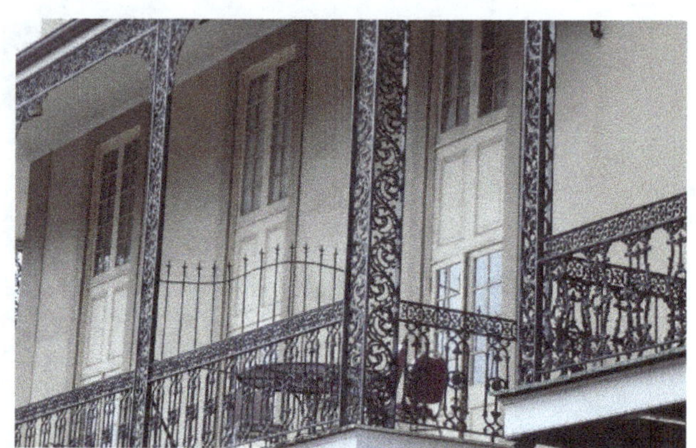
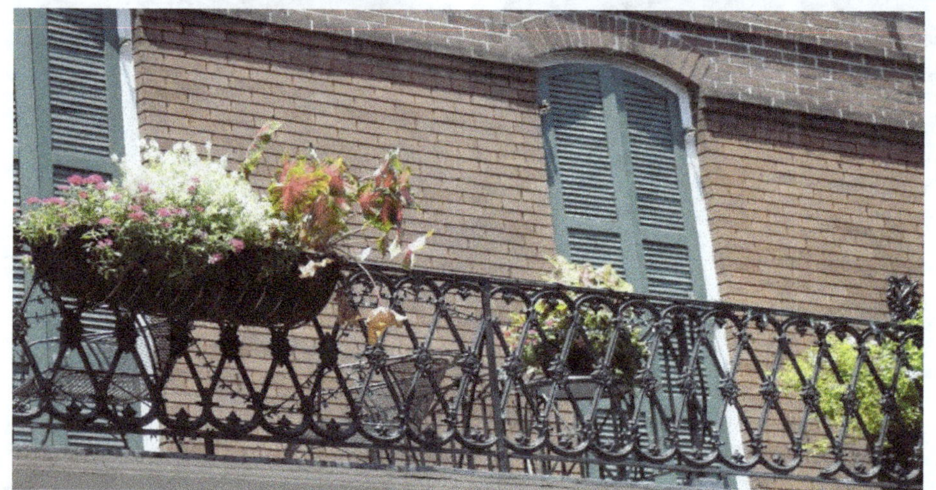
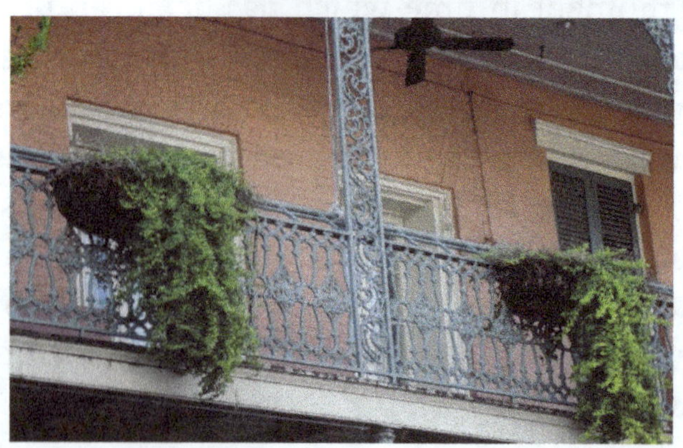
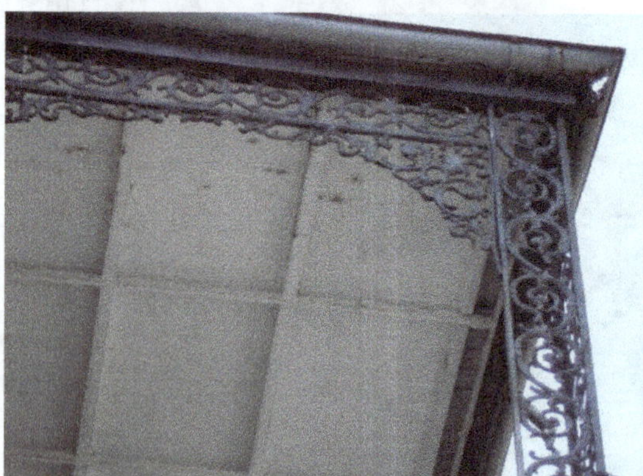

BIBLIOGRAPHY

Allured, Janet, and Judith F. Gentry. *Louisiana Women: Their Lives and times*. Athens, GA: U of Georgia, 2009. Print.

Bryant, Steve. *New Orleans: The Growth of the City*. Edison, NJ: Chartwell, 2007. Print.

Higgs, GM. *Anne Rice's Unauthorized French Quarter Tour Anne Rice Unauthorized Tours*. Cork: BookBaby, 2012. Print.

"History of Wrought Iron." *Wrought Iron Furniture and Iron Décor Store. N.p., n.d.* Web. 25 Jan. 2016.

King, David C. *New Orleans*. Brookfield, CT: Twenty-First Century, 1998. Print.

Lecoq, Raymond. *Classic French Wrought Iron*. New York: W.W. Norton, 2005, Print.

Martin, Eva Regina. *Forging from Sun-up to Sun-down: African Symbols in the Works of Black Ironworkers in New Orleans (1800-1863)*. N.p.: n.p., 1995. Print.

McKinney, Louise. *New Orleans: A Cultural History*. Oxford: Oxford UP, 2006. Print.

Vella, Christina. *The Baroness Pontalba*. N.p.: n.p., 1990. Print

Vella, Christina. Intimate Enemies: The Two Worlds of the Baroness De Pontalba. N.p.: Louisiana State UP, 2004. Print.